WHEN DRUGS HIT HOME

WHEN DRUGS HIT HOME

Lewis B. Hancock, Ph.D.

Shadow Mountain
Salt Lake City, Utah

Printed in the United States of America

Shadow Mountain is an imprint of Deseret Book Company

First printing October 1987

Library of Congress Cataloging-in-Publication Data

Hancock, Lewis B.
When drugs hit home/by Lewis B. Hancock
p. cm.

Includes index.
Summary: The director of a drug rehabilitation center discusses substance abuse by preteens and teens, pressures on youth and family, outside influences, how parents should react, strengths and weaknesses of available treatment programs and other aspects of drug use.
ISBN 0-87579-118-2
1. Youth—United States—Drug use. 2. Drug abuse—United States—Prevention. 3. Narcotic addicts—United States—Family relationships. 4. Parenting—United States. [1. Drug abuse.]
I. Title.
HV5824.Y68H36 1987 649'.4—dc19 87-22773

To the families of Dayspring

CONTENTS

ACKNOWLEDGMENTS

To all of the families who shared their stories for this book.

To Lynette Mecham and Jodee Brown, who lovingly and sensitively conducted the interviews of the families and wrote their stories.

To Emily Watts for all the editorial support and collaboration, without which this book would still be just an idea.

To Linda Cottam for her untiring commitment and positive attitude in typing the manuscript.

To the Dayspring staff for many conceptual contributions and their support in holding down the fort while I was writing.

To all the kids at Dayspring, who helped with many small vignettes and examples.

To my wife, Janetha, for always being there.

To God, who was my constant companion in writing this book and without whom there would be no answers.

Section 1

THE PROBLEM

Chapter 1

THE UNKNOWN PLAYER

It was November 20, 1983, and the holiday season was gaining momentum, glimmering through the streets of Salt Lake City. Laura was sitting at her desk, finalizing circulation lists for the December issue of a statewide magazine, when her phone rang. She stopped working, picked up the receiver, and struggled to understand her sixteen-year-old son's muddled words as they came tumbling over the line, punctuated by broken breathing.

Steve was crying. Something about trouble at school. Money for an art project. Talking back to his teacher. "Will they kick me out again? Will I have to go back to the juvenile detention center again? I couldn't stand that, Mom. What should I do? Please, can I call my girlfriend?"

Laura felt Steve's misery break over her in waves. He had been having a lot of problems lately with school, friends, and the law. But this time his pleading reminded her of a small, fearful bird, ready to fly but reluctant to leave the nest. Was it time to nudge him?

No, he couldn't call his girlfriend. She was in a drug rehabilitation program, and it wouldn't be fair to her. She was a nice girl, but drugs had really screwed up her life. Laura had worried at times about her influence on Steve but now felt confident that he was staying away from the drugs.

Laura felt a strange sense of foreboding in that conversation. She had felt that fear many times before. She knew that she should not try to rescue him as she had often done. That was part of his problem. Resolved, she reached down into her dwindling reserves of courage and reluctantly voiced her mentally rehearsed answer: "I guess you'll have to handle this yourself, Steve."

His words came back sounding hollow as empty seashells: "Okay, Mom, I'll handle this myself. And Mom . . . good-bye."

A short time later Laura's phone rang again. Steve was dead. Suicide. At home, with the family's handgun.

This scene is being played out more and more with our country's teenagers. Good kids, popular kids are dying at their own hands in ever greater numbers. The statistics are higher than anyone thought possible. How could teenagers who have so much to live for choose to end their lives? What could be causing such a tragedy? There is often an unknown player in this game of death.

The icy shadow that had threatened to smother Laura as she drove to her suburban home that afternoon would soon thicken into a cold, gray fog of guilt—a fog through which Laura would filter every subsequent memory of Steve and every question about his death. Was it her fault? How could this have happened? Her mind searched back through Steve's life. Had he been unusual? No, he had had a normal childhood. Was he unhappy as a child? No, only the last little while. Had he been confused? Maybe, especially the last two years. Everything seemed to have escalated when he became a teenager. Maybe it was the public school system. Maybe it was church. There must be an answer for this.

Laura would struggle for months before finding the unknown player in this senseless tragedy. The answer came from an unlikely source: after Steve's girlfriend was released from her rehabilitation program, she came to visit Laura. There was a feeling of penitence with her visit. Reluctantly she spoke of her and Steve's regular drug use. He had quit for only short periods. He had been very involved just before his death.

The hidden factor in Steve's problem—and thousands of others—was drugs. Thousands of parents this year will be catapulted into the realization that their kids are hooked on drugs. Most kids will use drugs for a year and a half to two years before their parents begin to detect it. Most will be daily users by the time their parents find out and take action. Most will have started in the seventh and eighth grades.

Every parent asks the same questions Laura did: How can this be? How could my kid use drugs right under my nose for so long? Could this really happen to my child? With luck, the crisis that brings us into realization of this problem will not be as tragic as Laura's.

Denial ran its course with Laura for months after Steve's death. Drugs? How could he use drugs without her detecting it? How could she have missed something so obvious? Was it her fault that he had used drugs? She came to me for counseling to resolve Steve's death and to find some way to prevent anything like it from ever happening again—she had a younger son, Stan, whom she was beginning to worry about.

A year after Steve's death Laura was beginning to feel more at peace, but Stan was beginning to show the same symptoms Steve had shown before his death. Stan's grades were slipping. He was skipping school. He began getting into trouble. He began reminding her of Steve.

No, she thought. Steve and Stan had always been different. Hadn't Steve been quieter, more reserved? Hadn't Stan established friendships more easily? Wasn't she imagining that Stan was suddenly taking on Steve's personality?

No, she thought again. Stan had always been active and goal oriented. Now he was listless and reactive. Nothing seemed to interest him anymore except having fun with his friends. Something was wrong. She watched the same hopelessness beckon Stan that had consumed her oldest son. The old wound was still scarring her family.

Laura refused to lose another child. She pushed back the comforting thoughts, the denial. It was denial that had convinced her that Steve (and now Stan) was just experiencing normal teenage tension. But this tension was not normal. She would do something for Stan. She would sit in the middle of the street and scream, if she had to. This time, she would find help.

Laura started coming in to see me again. As the profile

began to fall into place, I asked, "Is Stan using drugs?" Laura shook her head. "No. He may have tried marijuana, but nothing more," she answered. She was worried but felt that she was watching him closely enough to know if he was using.

I had done some investigating. As director of Dayspring, a chemical dependency treatment center for adolescents in Salt Lake City, I work with over a hundred kids in treatment. Through these connections I found that there was very little question that Stan had a serious drug and alcohol problem.

It took Laura several more weeks to work through her denial enough to bring Stan in for a two-day evaluation at Dayspring. Stan denied any problem at all, but two days of probing questions by Stan's peers, all of whom were users, brought a confession. Yes, he was using. How often? Daily. How serious was it? Stan was an addict.

Stan began intensive treatment in June 1985. He resisted being called an addict or an alcoholic. He had relapses, but Laura saw improvement every day. Stan's counselors were reaching him. His peers probed and prodded him relentlessly. The reverse peer pressure was intense and reached into areas that no adult could have explored. For the first time, Stan cried for his brother's death—the hurt, the fear, and the shame spilling outside him where they could be treated and healed.

The program treated drug use as a family disease—if one member of the family is sick, the family is sick. If drugs own one child, they own the entire household. The family attended dozens of meetings aimed at increasing awareness of the problem and improving relationships in the whole family. Stan continued with slow but steady progress each week.

The program addressed the lack of open communication between Laura and Greg, a problem that had threatened their marriage in its early years. They learned to abandon power struggles in favor of open communication. They addressed the faulty family dynamics that had resulted in each member feeling angry, misunderstood, and alienated at one time or another. They learned to approach problems with listening ears and hearts instead of blaming each other. Slowly Laura began to see through the guilt that had blocked her view into a universe of possibilities.

One meeting each week was especially powerful. It included all the kids in treatment and their families. The kids in the program sat on one side of the room looking back at their families, who sat on the other. The kids took turns presenting their drug histories and citing the harmful effects their use had had on their lives and families. It was in this meeting, watching and listening to other teens tell their stories, that Laura saw her lost son, Steve, by the light of his own reality.

Had drugs really been the hidden player in Steve's death? She began to ask. School counselors said they had wondered. Neighbors said they had thought so. Friends said yes. How often? Every day. For how long? At least two years before his suicide.

How had she and Greg felt so safe? she wondered. Hadn't they had discussions about drugs and alcohol? Hadn't they been good about not overreacting when their kids showed signs of an occasional party? They had both grown up in an area where social drinking was perfectly acceptable—and they had matured through it with no problems. But drugs? They'd skipped that era completely.

She remembered an incident when Steve was in the eighth grade. Steve's teacher had suspected Steve of smoking marijuana. He had called the principal, who had called in the police. Steve had collapsed in tears, utterly humiliated, when the police had smelled his hair. "I'd been eating apple taffy," he'd told his parents, whose fear now began fueling their anger.

"Don't you ever do that to our son without us here," they'd told the principal. They had believed Steve. They had hoped he now felt their support, felt better about trusting them.

As Laura watched hundreds of young people present their tragic stories in the family meetings, the picture became more and more clear. Their lives had been out of control, helplessly spiraling down toward the same end as Steve's. But these kids had a chance to be given a hand up, to stop that deadly spiral. Not all would accept the help, but Stan would, and for them that was what counted the most.

Laura looks now at the photograph hanging prominently in the entry hall of her home. It was taken two weeks before Steve's death, a Christmas surprise from daughter Kathryn. Laura smiles. Three young faces smile back at her. On the left, the tentative corners of Steve's mouth reach up toward his eyes. The brown curls at the base of his neck touch his collar. In the center, Kathryn's blond hair halos a face bright with confidence. On the right, Stan peers out directly, the zipper on his jacket slipped down a defiant inch or two below the top.

Laura will not see Steve's face again in this life, but her family is healing. Stan graduated from treatment after more than a year. He is doing well, but with this disease it will be a daily struggle for a long time to come. He is fortunate because he has a second chance—a chance to make things different. Communication is better now between Laura and Greg, between parents and kids. There is less explaining and more nurturing. But there are still fears, questions.

Laura thinks back on the question she asked so many times of so many others: "What's wrong with Steve?" Years of personal struggle and hours of intensive treatment have given Laura new insight into questions like these.

"What's wrong with Steve?" If she could pull him from the photograph now, hold his hands, and look into his smoky blue eyes, she would ask a question subtly, but significantly, different. "What's wrong, Steve?" she would say—patient, hopeful, and with an unwavering wisdom to wait as long as it took to hear his truth, knowing now to watch for that unknown player in this game of life and death.

Chapter 2

THE PROBLEM

The dog barked, waking Corinne Shelton to another sound. Someone was pounding on her front door. The bedroom clock said 3:00 A.M., but she was jolted from drowsiness into alarm at the sight of her eleven-year-old daughter, Jennifer, standing on the porch next to a police officer.

"I found Jennifer wandering in the park," the officer said. "I think she may be high."

Corinne watched Jennifer move across the living room with the exaggerated, dreamlike gestures of the sloth monkey at the zoo. "Are you on something?" she asked, a little angry and a lot afraid.

"No, Mom," Jennifer answered.

Corinne had never considered herself a naive mother. She knew that police officers brought teenagers home to their parents far too often. But she also knew that this scenario held one shocking distinction: Jennifer was not a teenager. Jennifer was barely eleven years old, a sixth grader at a suburban elementary school. The officer had to be wrong. Didn't he?

"I'm going to take you to the doctor later today and have your urine tested for drugs," Corinne told Jennifer as she sent her daughter to bed.

"That's okay, Mom. They won't find anything," Jennifer answered, her pseudosad voice communicating that she clearly felt she was the most oppressed child in all of daughterdom.

"I had to be at work at the post office at 5:30 that

morning," Corinne remembers. "But I called the school counselor and then made an appointment with Jennifer's doctor. He took a urine sample, and we waited for two weeks for the results of the scan. Jennifer hardly spoke to me during those two weeks. I was totally convinced that she had been telling the truth and that I had done terrible things to her dignity. I was sure I had damaged our relationship permanently."

The results of the urine test were a shock. The scan revealed traces of alcohol, barbiturates, and THC (the chemical found in marijuana). Jennifer had been using for several months without anyone being able to detect it—until now. She had been involved in thefts, vandalism, and some dealing. She had begun daily use and had even gotten to the point of shooting up drugs intravenously—drugs that she did not even know the names of. Jennifer was an addict.

We have a problem—and it is reaching alarming proportions. We see it daily on the television. The president's wife, the governor's wife, and more and more celebrities are speaking out in public against it. Yet, even with all this, we have somehow been deceived into believing that the drug-abuse problem of the sixties is getting better.

Society has traditionally perceived drug abuse as a college student problem. Surely, we think, this is not something we need to worry about with our youth. Consequently, over the past twenty years we have become increasingly numb to the intrusion of drugs into senior high, junior high, and even elementary school populations. Recent studies have shown that drug and alcohol use is ten times greater than parents typically suspect.

Drugs have become much stronger and more prevalent over the past two decades. In 1972 the average age at which a person first tried drugs was fifteen. By 1986 the average age of first use had dropped to twelve. Almost 20 percent of our teenagers have a drinking problem. The number of graduating high school seniors who have used cocaine is 41 percent, more than twice what it was in 1975. Peer pressure has mounted with junior high and high school students to a point that someone who has never tried alcohol or drugs is truly seen as a geek, a nerd, or a goody-two-shoes.

Parents get tired of worrying about the constant threats of alcohol and drugs to their kids. The pervasiveness of the problem has brought them to the saturation point of fear, and consequently many have become numb to its implications. Even parents who grew up during the sixties and who saw drug abuse in its infancy do not understand the ramifications of nine-, ten-, and eleven-year-olds using drugs regularly. Cases like Jennifer's are becoming more common every day.

Jennifer's drug history, though alarming because of her age, followed some fairly classic patterns. Jennifer's father, grandfather, and aunt were alcoholics, and Jennifer often observed her father drunk. In fact, Jennifer's first experience with alcohol came from tasting her father's drinks, though Corinne is sure he would never have allowed that if he had been sober. And with the marriage deteriorating under Corinne's feet, Jennifer often observed her mother struggling to fend off blows to her own self-esteem. With her husband gone, Corinne was left to support the kids, Jennifer and Kevin. As a result, Jennifer's drug use went largely unobserved.

But there are dimensions to Jennifer's history that seem harder to reconcile with drug use. Jennifer looks out of large brown eyes set in a clear, lightly tanned face with the features of a teen model. Her hair is the color of freshly shelled chestnuts. She is bright, playful, energetic, and sweet.

"I guess I was popular at school in a way," she says. "When I was ten, my boyfriend was fifteen. People always thought I was in high school. In elementary school my twin friends (also users) and I frightened the other kids. They would part for us when we walked down the hall. But, to me, being feared and respected was a kind of popularity."

Jennifer exhibits a shrewd street sense and a sort of hyperconfidence. This bravado may have helped propel her, from age nine, into the dangerous sorts of mischief usually associated with late-evening television dramas. At age ten, Jennifer became part of a gang that met in an abandoned train station to plan fights. She vandalized churches. She robbed cars and homes. And she used marijuana, alcohol, and cross-top speed almost every day. These risks were "fun" and helped her avoid her heartaches.

How did Jennifer get these drugs? And where did she get the money to buy them?

"There are dealers in every school," Jennifer says. "And you don't have to have a lot of money. You just have to be willing to share what you have. Even if all you can come up with sometimes is your lunch money, you can get drugs.

"It's like any close school crowd," she continues, "except, unlike other crowds, you don't have to have special qualities to belong. You don't have to be rich. You don't have to be pretty. You don't have to be athletic. You don't have to be smart or have a great personality. You just have to do drugs."

As parents, we need to understand that the world we grew up in has, to a large extent, disappeared. High technology and mobility have changed the structure of our families, our schools, and our lives and have made our children much more vulnerable to drug and alcohol abuse. Recognizing these changes is an important step in understanding what our youth are up against.

Changes in the Family

Parents today face many child-rearing challenges that were unknown forty years ago—or even ten years ago. When we were growing up, things were slower. Life was less complex than it is today. Our society was moving out of an agrarian age into a more highly specialized industrial age.

When most Americans lived in rural areas and grew up on farms, people were much less mobile. They stayed home more, and they settled much closer to home to take up their professions. Consequently, extended families were much closer. Grandpa and Grandma lived down the street. Aunt Mary and Uncle Fred lived around the corner.

We all went to the same church and would see many of the family and community at least once a week. Today Grandpa and Grandma have divorced. Grandma is living in Arizona, and Grandpa has moved to California, and we've moved three times in the last ten years.

The breakdown of the extended family has left parents very vulnerable. We have few other surrogate parent role models for our children to bond to and learn from. We have little help enforcing the rule systems we set for our families or carrying through with family traditions. The process of intervention into a problem has changed. It used to be that a great many family members could be brought together to confront a problem. A mischievous young person could be confronted at every turn as he walked down the street by a neighbor, a grocer, or a gas station attendant who knew the child well. Now we can hide for months at a time without seeing anyone we recognize; we protect ourselves and our children from anyone else's corrective feedback.

The nuclear family is the core of the strength of our society; however, when the immediate family is isolated and removed from the extended family, it can become weakened and vulnerable to problems such as drug abuse. Divorce over the past couple of decades has gone far beyond our wildest nightmares. Recent studies of American marriage show that in only one out of ten marriages would both partners rank their marriage as very satisfactory. The whole structure of the family has changed: only 17 percent of American families are traditional two-parent families with the mother remaining full-time in the home. For good or bad, the influencing of our children has been left in the hands of people other than parents.

During World War II women went to work for the country. They established themselves as a viable work force and enjoyed the respect they gained from bringing home paychecks. Innovations, tools, and appliances for managing a home have skyrocketed in the last two decades. Mom doesn't need to spend a day and a half each week doing the laundry, or five to six hours a day preparing food. These factors have contributed to more and more two-career families. It follows logically, then, that the amount of time children spend with family members, and especially with parents, has been reduced significantly. Research has shown that if the hours of adult supervision of a child are reduced, the incidence of alcohol and drug use will rise.

Schools

Today's school systems are another aspect of our rapidly changing society that has made us increasingly vulnerable to drug abuse. It used to be that parents were able to know their children's teachers personally. As society has grown and schools have become more specialized, teachers have also had to specialize. At younger and younger grades now our children are moved into multiple classes with multiple teachers. They are getting more specialized knowledge but are losing the ability to bond and build close relationships with a few people. This process parallels the breakdown of the extended family and also precipitates drug abuse among our young people. I have often wondered whether the specialized knowledge is worth our children's growing up with much less meaningful relationships with their teachers. When a teacher is trying to teach 150 students in a day, it becomes almost impossible for that teacher to develop any long-term relationships with individual children. As a result, children start turning to the only people they know and trust and spend a lot of time with each day: their peers.

Children today also have much more freedom in school than in former years. Campuses are generally open, and many kids have cars and can come and go at will. No one is directly responsible for seeing that a teen gets to class, so it's easy to slip through the cracks. All these factors combine to create a fertile environment for drug abuse, and, indeed, schools are a hotbed of drug activity.

Entertainment and the Media

Another area of change in our highly technical and specialized society is the growth in the entertainment industry. We often point to the media as the primary culprit in eroding our family system. It is only one factor in many, but it does make its special contributions. The fact that today we can come home to lifelike, colorful, moving pictures and have our choice from hundreds of alternatives of entertainment has made TV an integral part of our lives. The home that does not have a TV on sometime during the day is the extremely rare exception. Most of our living rooms have now been built to face toward the television set. Few of us have (or would use) rooms where the furniture is set up in a circle to induce conversation. Front porches on homes, which used to encourage neighborhood interaction, have been virtually eliminated in favor of backyard decks behind the seclusion of nice, solid fences. Our level of interaction within the family and within our neighborhoods has dropped significantly. We have exchanged live associates for animated ones.

An interesting experiment to try some night would be to disable the television set and see what family members did to occupy their time. For many this would be a family crisis. Most of us, however, would just drag out the second set and continue on with our nightly routine. The one-eyed monster provides a deceptive feeling of the warmth of a house full of life. If you don't believe that, turn the set off sometime and just feel the change in mood. For some it brings on panic, for others a welcome relief. But without the allure of the TV, family members' common reaction is to gravitate to their own rooms or over to friends' houses rather than to communicate with one another.

Some treatment programs employ a weekend retreat format where family members are required to go into a motel room without a television set. They are not allowed to leave the room and are forced to interact with each other for an entire weekend. Invariably this will bring about a major crisis for the first couple of hours. Just as predictably, however, when the weekend is over, it will go down in that family's history as one of the most significant events they have ever gone through. Unfortunately, the family will probably then go home, relax, flip on the TV, and forget about the experience for several months.

Advertising and Instant Gratification

Another contribution of media to the problem of drug abuse falls in the lap of the advertisement industry. Billions of dollars are generated each year by products aimed to give us—immediately—whatever our hearts desire. For example, all of us have experienced the convenience-store explosion. I can scarcely drive five blocks in my city without coming across a convenience store where I can slide in and pick up something to fill immediately my need for gratification. We have fast food and fast credit, and we are quickly teaching ourselves that anything that has to be waited for can't be worth having. Instant gratification is at the heart of drug abuse; it is a philosophy with frightening implications. The older and wiser we get, the more clearly we can see that the things that really gratify us and give us meaning are those things that take a long time and a lot of work to obtain.

Our teenagers are convinced that we adults have sold out to the system, that we gave up too quickly to a life of drudgery. They do not understand the work ethic; they think we ended up working because we couldn't come up with a more creative way to achieve our goals. They feel that there really is a utopian existence out there where you can have everything and have it right now with no consequences. They believe that if we would just dream a little and not get so hung up in our conservativism, we could really experience a fulfilling life. Their songs are filled with rebellious lyrics, sometimes idealistic, sometimes cynical. They are convinced that such things as falling in love and fighting the system are the ultimate end—despite how little they actually know about being in love or living in this competitive world.

Make a survey of current movies sometime. The great majority deal with some sort of falling-in-love scenario and typically end with either a happy or a tragic result. When was the last time you saw a movie that featured two people who had already fallen in love long since and were now dealing with the realistic journey of learning how to truly love one another over a period of time? Try to think of one in which people actually went off to work. No one would pay good money to watch a movie about marriage or jobs; it wouldn't be romantic enough. And yet, for those of us who have found a best friend, a true companion, or a job that we really like, the satisfaction far outweighs the allure of a short-term high or escape.

Movement toward More Permissive Values

Another major contribution of the media to our changing society is an amoral stance toward life. No matter how much we may disagree with it, the movement in the media has been toward teaching a value system more permissive than the one we grew up with. When was the last time you saw a sexual encounter on TV or in the movies between two married people? And yet it's next to impossible to go to a movie or to watch television today without seeing some sort of sexual encounter between two unmarried people.

We might as well accept the fact that our children are going to grow up in a much more permissive society than we would wish. On the positive side, such a society provides a chance for our children to make a clear, conscious decision about which direction they want to go in life. Our job is to make sure they can objectively sort through the lies and find the truth within the media. They must learn to understand the consequences of different actions. They need to know that drugs, alcohol, sex, and breaking the law all have inescapable consequences. The ultimate choice, however, they must make themselves. They have to make their own decisions—and take their own lumps.

God made free agency a necessary part of our existence here, and we cannot take away that right or responsibility. What we can hope to do is delay those decisions until the point when a child has all the facts and can make a good, conscious decision.

Influence of Peers

To sum up, our kids live in a society in which the extended family has been virtually eliminated, Mom has been removed from the home, schools have become more sterile, entertainment options have skyrocketed, instant gratification has become a way of life, and societal values have loosened considerably. It becomes clear why peers have such a significant and unhealthy influence over teenagers today.

The word *teenager* didn't even appear in the vocabulary until around the time of World War II. It used to be that those teenage years were seen as a preparation time for adulthood. Now they are seen as a big, blank space. Nothing that teenagers do seems to be relevant in their preparation for adulthood. Consequently, they feel as if their teen years are their last time of freedom, their golden age, their chance to party and have a good time while being supported by their parents.

As one teenager said as he was being checked into our treatment program, "I can't spend the summer in a rehab program. Come on, Mom! This is the last summer that I will get to have a good time. Pretty soon I'll have to move out and get a job, and I won't have the time or money to enjoy myself. My friends and I have lots of parties planned. I can't believe you expect for me to give that up to be cooped up in this program." It is amazing to see how perceptive the kids can be about their situation and yet at the same time have no appreciation for what their parents have given them.

In countless interviews with chemically dependent teenagers, I have found that they aren't worried about flunking out of school, about losing their families, or even about close-to-death experiences. What they are the most concerned about is that we are going to rob them of the last chance they will have to party before having to become adults. They do not like anyone to remind them of the real world that faces them in only a few short years.

The more they can stay away from their parents and around their peers, the better off they feel that they are. Parents pose a serious threat: they've seen the teen's greatest faults, and they are a constant reminder that the kid is supposed to be preparing for adulthood. Peers seldom pose that threat. Peers provide an atmosphere of immediate acceptance with few membership criteria and few initial expectations. The teenager is also able to start fresh with the new group.

Many teen peer groups are formed on a strong foundation of rebellion and righteous indignation toward the adult world. Adolescence is a period of stretching limits to see just how far you can go. All of us have been enticed by the thought of bagging all our values and letting things run at full throttle—just to see what it is like. Many teenagers are trying to do just that.

American businesses spend billions of dollars to make sure that those opportunities exist for teenagers. As parents, we continue to make those businesses lucrative by providing our children with incomes without making them account for where they spend the money. Consequently, our teens continue to control the movie industry, the music industry, the fast food industry, and so on. They have convinced themselves that we adults have completely missed the boat. They turn to peers for advice on major life issues, hoping to have their utopian conceptions confirmed and validated. The problem is that most of these peers could fit their real-life experience in a thimble. It is not until years later—after suffering the hard knocks of the real world and alienating themselves from their families—that these kids realize that their parents and the adults in their lives may have been giving wiser advice than they knew.

Most of us as parents have become so busy with our own lives that we have difficulty trying to keep up with the peers in our children's lives. Do you know who your children's friends are? Do you have those peers in your home frequently? Do you know who the parents of those peers are? These are some of the first requirements for parents whose kids are in drug treatment. Our kids are so mobile today that if we don't make a concerted effort to get to know their friends, they can quickly get involved in a new friendship system that we have no knowledge of.

It's always interesting to me that I can go to neighbors, schoolteachers, and other people who are loosely associated with our children and have them tell me in a moment what kind of peers a certain kid has. Yet often when I interview the parents, I find that they have very little idea who their own child's friends are. Parents need to shake off their complacency in this area and understand that the strongest research predictor of drug abuse among children is whether or not their friends are users.

Everyone's Problem

Yes, we have a problem, and no family, no matter how strong, is immune. Ask Frederick and Jan Barton, who at one time had two sons and a son-in-law in drug rehabilitation programs. Not so unusual—except that Frederick was Metropolitan Narcotics Strike Force commander in his city, and his kids "should have known better." Ask David and Jeanne Peterson, who had supported their son Craig in music, sports, church, and school activities all his life. Put yourself in the place of Richard and Heidi Randall. "If anyone had asked, I'd have told them I was the epitome of motherhood with a perfect little family," says Heidi. "So I sometimes wonder myself what happened." As you read the Randalls' story, ask yourself honestly if such a thing could happen to your family. Could it be happening right now?

Is Our Family Unique?

What qualities does the family have whose child becomes addicted to alcohol or drugs? Richard Randall wonders, paging mentally through the years before two of his sons became addicts/alcoholics and entered the Dayspring rehabilitation program. He looks at his boys now: Jim's dark hair, sharp, playful eyes, gregarious smile; Brett's feather-blond halo, his timid yet carefree style. Young men to whom girls would flock, to whom the elderly would entrust an arm for escort. Richard Randall's brow furrows. "Look at them," he pleads. "What made us unique? Is there a story here?"

I had known the Randalls and their good reputation in the community for years. Richard, a department store owner, had served for over twenty years as a congregational and area leader in his church. Heidi chaired our county's commission on youth. I had served on the commission for a couple of years and was always impressed with the way her savvy leadership combined with a genuine gentleness and caring.

The Randalls' kitchen table would unite seven family members for dinner. Their plaid couch, fireplace, and plush-pile rug were the setting for weekly scripture readings and moral teachings. The recreation industry could count on the Randall clan every Monday evening for an activity as part of their spiritual life. And the local church had all but reserved a pew for them. Theirs was a healthy family, one that most people would suppose to be protected against chemical dependency.

Heidi Randall warned her children that alcohol addiction was a disease that ran in her family. She explained that this was the most critical reason they should be leery of taking a drink. But Jim disregarded her advice. "It was about eighth grade," says Jim. "I had a lot of friends—we weren't jocks, but we weren't the stoners either. We just kind of hung around together, cut class a little, and muddled our way through. Pot and beer were big all over the school, so when I was offered some, I decided to try it."

His curiosity soon gave way to a sporting pastime. Smoking pot and drinking beer were Jim's way to have fun on weekends. "Mom and Dad never knew because I'd wait a couple hours after drinking before I'd come home. If my eyes were red, I'd put Visine in them. Sometimes we'd even smoke at school, before my church seminary class, but the teacher never seemed to know either. And my parents knew that all the kids I hung around with were good kids, too. We were, really."

When Jim graduated to high school, the "stuff" became easier to find. So did places and opportunities to use it: unguarded bathrooms, certain hallways, the locker room, parking lots, and even some classrooms.

Heidi and Richard were kept in the dark. Jim continued to bring home passing grades and play on the varsity tennis team, both perfect camouflages for his increasingly disruptive behavior. Sure, Jim was becoming a little hostile. Fights about staying out too late led to doors slamming, voices blaring, and punishment ensuing. But to his parents, he was simply rebelling—breaking away—finding a life of his own. Were the alcohol on his breath and the smell of smoke on his clothes dead giveaways, or, as Jim insisted, just an innocent swallow of beer and a cigarette bummed from a friend? For Heidi and Richard, there was fear but always hope. Always good rationalizations. And lots of denial.

Things began to deteriorate. Lying increased, grades dropped, and family life was full of conflict. "By the time I hit college I was using all the time. Mom would tell me to straighten up or move out. So I'd move out. Then I'd lose my job, run out of money, and move back in, promising to straighten up my act. But I couldn't."

Heidi's son couldn't change. By this time, she thought she knew why. But could a few cigarettes and a little alcohol make her son so irresponsible? And if they could, how could she stop it? He fought against her help and anyone else's whenever the subject came up.

Richard, frequently out of town on business, listened as Heidi sobbed over the telephone. He wondered, could it be so bad? Why couldn't she take a hard line with the boy? He did when he was home. And what could he do? Should he quit his job so he'd be home all the time for a boy who was old enough to be on his own now? His other kids seemed to be fine. He loved Jim. He'd do anything for him. But what would really help? His work as an LDS stake president was for his church. Wouldn't God help?

Brett Gets into the Picture

Brett was a great kid. He was always involved in family activities. He took leadership roles in church. He was an Eagle Scout. He carried a very high grade point average in school. Brett's quiet sincerity had always won his parents' favor. But his bashful demeanor had not won favor with himself. He wanted to equal his older brother—to be worldly and wise, have lots of friends, and always have a good time.

Brett was quick to catch up with his brother. While it took Jim a good seven years to foul up his life with drugs and alcohol, it took Brett only months.

It started with some beer he was offered at a movie. It progressed to getting drunk at the junior high school dances. Then Brett got caught. The principal called his parents and asked them to come down and get him.

"I was ashamed because I'd let my parents down," says Brett. "I loved my parents and decided to quit." And he did, for a while. The next summer at church camp, some of the guys caught him smoking. "I remember getting into my suitcase," says Brett. "All my cigarettes were crumpled in little pieces all over my clothes. The kids had all walked out and left me alone. I don't know what they wanted to prove, but it made me mad, and I left camp."

He left not only camp but also his commitment to keep away from drugs and alcohol. Within a month he was getting high daily. His grades fell. Within four more months, Brett was following in his brother's footsteps.

Intervention and Treatment

"When the boys would make trouble, we'd inflict punishments," says Heidi, still trying to identify her role in their downfall. "When they weren't home on time, I'd chase them down. When I suspected they were smoking or drinking, I'd stand over them and hound them about it. If they didn't seem to care, I'd talk to them—love them out of it." She throws her arms in the air. "If nothing else, I kept my kids' brains active in guessing what tack I'd take next."

The Randalls were caught up in despair. They'd watched Jim slip away, and now Brett was headed toward the same fate.

Trying one more tactic, Heidi made an appointment for Brett to come and see us at Dayspring. We suggested he have a two-day evaluation. "It was a scare tactic, that's all," Heidi remembers. "He didn't have a real problem. Not compared to Jim, and not as far as I was ready to admit."

I asked Brett to evaluate his problem on a scale of one to ten. Brett answered "J," for not-in-the-running. But after two days Brett changed his mind. He was going to stay. Why? "The kids asked me one question I couldn't come to grips with," he says. "They asked me what the chances were I'd stop drinking and taking drugs. I said, 'no chance.' I had no desire to quit. It was the first time I'd ever thought of it that way. But I needed my drugs to get by."

Another Chance for Jim

After several months of treatment Brett was becoming wise to the strain drugs had placed on his family as well as on himself. He had also assigned himself the task of bringing his older brother down off drugs. Brett wrote a speech. He read it to Jim through a locked bathroom door. The words were soft with Brett's tears. Jim listened impassively at first, not hearing, not believing. Hardened. The words gnawed at Jim's conscience, however, and it wasn't long until the second miracle happened. Jim entered treatment.

Together they have supported each other in the daily struggle to stay straight and healthy. As they complete their treatment they know that the threat of relapse will be ever present. Alcoholics Anonymous and Narcotics Anonymous meetings have become a way of life.

As Jim leaves for a meeting, Heidi's jaw tightens. "He's twenty-two years old. I shouldn't have to worry about him. But I do. If he uses again, he's dead on the streets." Tears well in her eyes.

"We have to remember," Richard places a hand on his wife's hand and repeats the words they learned in treatment meetings, "we didn't cause it; we can't cure it; we can only work our own program and let our higher power do the rest." Then he shakes his head. "Even as I say those words, I still get a knot in my stomach," he says. One arm around his father's shoulder, Brett repeats his words, "But you didn't cause it; you can't cure it; we can only accept it and go on from here."

Chapter 3

THE DISEASE CONCEPT

Nine of Philip's relatives have died from alcoholism. Philip might have been number ten. But the car accident that could have killed him was the eye-opener that saved him.

The moon was dim, the streets were dark, and the banks of the canyon were lined with snow that crisp November night. But Philip was hot—winning a game of cat-and-mouse chase in his parents' car. "They're gaining on us," yelled his friend, who was sitting on the passenger side. Philip sat upright, clutched the steering wheel, and floored the gas pedal. "That's okay, I don't have it into fifth yet," he said, reaching for the gearshift and glancing at the speedometer. It was reaching seventy.

They were approaching Suicide Rock at the entrance to Parley's Canyon when the car from behind finally slipped to the side of Philip's car, tagged the front end, and zipped ahead.

Trying to recover, Philip jerked the wheel. But his car hit the inside guardrail, shot west to the outside guardrail, turned on its side, and stopped just inches short of a two-hundred-foot drop-off.

Philip could hear his heart pounding in the still air of 2:00 A.M. He could feel blood running down his throat and the grit of glass crunching in his teeth. He could see blood seeping from his T-shirt, and his buddy lying limp, but awake, against the passenger door, which was smashed into the road. His first thoughts were only to climb out and check on the damages to his parents' car.

Minutes later, a passerby stopped to help and called the police. Philip and his buddy were rushed to the hospital, where they were bandaged, X-rayed, and tested for, among other things, blood alcohol levels.

Vicki and Cliff Sorensen were vacationing in a neighboring state when they received a phone call the next evening. It was Philip, their son. "I could tell he was upset when he told me the car was wrecked," says Vicki. "But I could also tell there was more. Then he told me he'd got a DUI (ticket for driving under the influence of alcohol) but that the blood report revealed his alcohol level had been only .06 (.08 is legally drunk). My heart sank."

Vicki knew the odds are low for getting a DUI after the first time of drinking, so she asked, hesitantly, "How long has this been going on, Philip?"

"Two years," he answered. Uneasy silence followed.

Vicki scrambled for clues, her mind researching episodes from the past two years. Philip would have been sixteen, only a sophomore, when he'd begun drinking. Sure, his grades had started slipping that year, and he had seemed somewhat depressed. But Philip had never been an outspoken person—he had always kind of kept to himself. And they'd even tried to work on that by taking Philip to a counselor and getting his I.Q. checked, which proved to be around 130—high enough for him to do almost anything he wanted. He sat in church with the family every Sunday. He was always home on time, always seemed responsible. He'd run some good races and competed in triathlons. And he'd played terrific basketball. . . . Of course, of course, this DUI was one of those freaky adolescent things that all kids get caught up in. And the two years of drinking—it was surely one of those phases.

Regaining confidence, Vicki continued the conversation with Philip, calmly helping him reason the facts and consequences of his accident and suggesting the name of a lawyer he should get in touch with tomorrow—also stressing that they would talk more about it when she and Cliff got home.

She hung up the phone. The fears resurfaced. Something wasn't right. She'd felt it for the past two years, and now—well, maybe this was it. Maybe her Philip, the one kid in the family whom she had thought she wouldn't have to worry about, just maybe he was caught in a dreadful family pattern. Four of Cliff's sisters and two of his brothers had died of alcoholism. Her own grandfather, and then father, had died alcohol-related deaths. And just recently, her cousin had died at age fifty. Alcohol was the cause.

Chemical dependency is a disease. Cases like Philip's, which point out strong genetic determinants, help confirm this concept. But when I first started working with alcoholics and drug addicts I had a hard time believing it. My professional schooling had taught me that drug and alcohol abuse were typically symptoms of some underlying problem. As my experience progressed, it became clear to me that there was something here that was more than just a symptom.

The abuse of chemicals must be seen by therapists and parents as the primary problem that must be handled first. It doesn't matter what changes are made in the family, what progress teenagers might make with self-image or other life skills; if the chemical dependency is not addressed specifically, it will tear down any progress made in any other direction. Improvement in those lateral areas is essential during treatment, but many counselors do not specifically address the disease of chemical dependency.

Many parents have trouble viewing drug addiction as a disease because of the aspect of choice involved. While it is true that kids do choose initially to experiment with drugs, the great majority of them would not choose to be chemically dependent. By the time teenagers reach their senior year, more than 90 percent will have done some experimenting with alcohol or drugs. Approximately 10 percent will go on to have significant problems with chemical abuse.

There is an intricate combination of variables that can determine whether a child becomes chemically dependent. It can happen to anyone, but some people are predisposed to it, like time bombs waiting to go off. Many times, as in Philip's case, addiction is genetic. Studies show conclusively that if you have chemical dependency among your ancestors, your children will have a three to five times greater chance of becoming chemically dependent themselves. Many kids have a psychological makeup that will lead them toward chemical dependency more quickly. Some are just unfortunate in the drugs they pick: a child who gets into cocaine or painkillers, which are fast-acting drugs, will become addicted much more quickly than a child who uses marijuana, a fairly slow-acting drug. Research also proves that the earlier a person starts to use drugs or alcohol, the greater is that person's chance of becoming addicted. This is the main problem today with chemical dependency among our youth. They are using drugs at earlier and earlier ages, and hence run a much greater risk of becoming chemically dependent.

Many parents feel a tremendous amount of resentment when their children abuse drugs. They might blame the child's friends or some unseen drug dealer who has seduced their kid into a life of crime. They also feel a lot of guilt, as though their child's problems were all their fault. But children have to make choices, and unfortunately, in this day and age, most kids are going to choose to experiment with drugs. Many will develop the disease of chemical dependency. We must face that fact and be willing to deal with it.

The disease of chemical dependency has four qualities: it is primary, progressive, chronic, and fatal. It affects the entire being of the person who has it. The best thing about chemical dependency, when compared to other potentially fatal diseases, is that it can be arrested. We do have treatment that works.

Most medical problems today—most heart disease, lung disorders, and gastrointestinal disorders—are caused by things related to our life-style. Chemical dependency is caused the same way. Our job as parents and professionals is to stop the disease, bring about treatment, and educate our children to the natural consequences they will encounter if they continue to abuse. After that, it does become an issue of choice. Then the children must make very serious choices and make them better than they did previously. After we have done everything we can, if our children choose not to make the life-style change, they will suffer the same consequences as a lung cancer patient who continues to smoke, a person with heart disease who continues to drink, or a diabetic who persists in poor nutritional habits.

Kids from all walks of life can develop the disease of chemical dependency, but once they have it, the progression is very similar in all cases. The disease can be broken into four stages, the end of which is death. These stages are experimentation, preoccupation, dependence, and disintegration.

Stage One: Experimentation

As mentioned earlier, almost all kids in the United States will experiment at one time or another with mood-altering chemicals. For most, the initiation comes through peer pressure. More experienced users who have learned how to change their moods through the use of drugs encourage their nonusing friends to try them. First use generally occurs around the seventh or eighth grade and will usually be with alcohol, marijuana, or inhalants. Many kids report that during their first use they felt no mood change at all. Very few have a bad experience with their first use, so immediately they begin to doubt the things that have been taught them about the harmful effects of drugs. Having now been initiated into the club, the child can more easily justify further drug-use episodes.

Beyond that, a more powerful stimulus takes over. The drugs will soon start to have an effect, and the child will learn to respond to the euphoria they provide. With a sense of having partaken of forbidden fruit, the child realizes that drugs really are fun. Often when speaking to groups the kids will be asked why they used drugs the first time. "Because they are fun," many reply. "I used because my friends all use. To be able to fit in I went ahead and tried them. But after I tried them I really liked the effects." The feeling of the drug becomes better and better to the child.

Here is a whole new experience that seems to be beckoning him or her into a world never before discovered. With a sense of adventure and only a few apprehensions the teenager moves into Stage Two of the disease.

Stage Two: Preoccupation

In Stage Two adolescents begin to actively seek out the effects of the drugs and plan their use. They can move rapidly from occasional experimentation to using at least once a week. They will feel some mild doubts and some gnawing guilt, but the experiential learning—the actual doing and feeling of drug use—far outweighs the power of what they have learned in discussions with their parents or at school or in church. So they forge on. At this point the drug use becomes premeditated, and deception must enter into the drug abuser's world. A little lie here and there seems a small price to pay for the euphoria that the drug user has begun to find. "My parents would never understand. They've never done drugs, so they can't understand what it would be like to actually use them. What they don't know can't hurt them." Experiential learning takes over again, as the kids find they can lie a great many times without getting caught. It truly seems that there is no problem as long as their parents or family don't find out.

At this point the most common pattern is for kids to use marijuana two or three times a week and alcohol whenever they can on the weekends. They soon find that the slow-acting effects of marijuana are much easier to conceal from parents than the effects of other drugs. At this stage of the disease, kids spend many hours discussing how to conceal their drug use from parents, teachers, and police. They also rationalize among themselves that their use is not really harmful. "Everybody is doing it. Some states have even legalized it. It won't be long until the whole country realizes that marijuana is just like alcohol and it should be legalized as well." Although some states have decriminalized marijuana, making possession of small amounts a misdemeanor instead of a felony, it is not actually legal anywhere in the United States. But kids will seize whatever evidence they can get. They pick out the most credible adults they can find to show that people can use marijuana and alcohol socially without having any problems.

The legality of alcohol is probably the number-one rationalization used by kids. "There just isn't anything wrong with having a beer once in a while. My Uncle Fred has one or two beers a month when he watches football games. Lots of states have dropped their drinking age to eighteen. The only reason they don't legalize it for the rest of us is they want to reserve the pleasure for themselves."

As Stage Two progresses, many teenagers go from using only at parties to beginning to use when they are by themselves. The mood swing is not quite as much fun without others to enjoy it with them, but it's equally predictable. One of the most powerful things about drugs and alcohol at this stage is that the effect is always predictable. There are very few things in life that a person can rely on to change his or her mood. Teenagers find a lot of security in the fact that they can turn back to drugs at any time with the reliable mood-changing effect. Another thing the teenager in Stage Two learns is that using drugs takes away thoughts of any problems he or she may have. It provides a great escape.

With regular use, teenagers will begin to develop a tolerance to some of the drugs. They may become bored with the effects of alcohol and marijuana, which are largely depressant drugs, and may begin to turn more toward stimulants and hallucinogens. It is at the end of Stage Two that the kids begin to experiment with other drugs such as speed, LSD, and possibly cocaine. As the tolerance begins to build, as the teenager becomes more and more preoccupied with the drug, and as the use becomes more regular, the teen begins to move into Stage Three, dependence.

Stage Three: Dependence

As Stage Three progressess, the teenager is using drugs more often to escape from stress. As tolerance begins to build, the teen has to use increasing amounts of the drug to achieve the same euphoria that was experienced in the beginning. Drug use will become a daily event. This is a critical step in the progression of the disease. When the child starts to use daily, the effects of one drug-using event overlap onto the next. The residue effects of hangovers and apathy syndrome are covered up by the use of more drugs. Stage Three users never quite recover from one episode before going on to the next. In fact, they quickly find that the best cure for a hangover is a drink or a joint.

The more the teenager escapes from his or her problems, the more they pile up. A typical scenario: Tim does not like school, so when Steve and Julie invite him to skip third period and go use with them, he grabs the chance. Every time he misses school, he gets further behind in his work. The further behind he gets, the more risk he runs of being confronted by his teachers, thus confirming his dislike of school. The worse his schoolwork gets, the greater the allure of slipping out and escaping through cutting class and using drugs. This pattern will propel Tim right out of school. When he is finally suspended, he has the freedom to use as much as he wants, and he falls still further behind in school. He is caught in a rapidly moving downward spiral.

The child who is getting deeper and deeper into trouble usually recognizes it and starts to feel some remorse: "How could I have been so stupid? I've been kicked out of school, my parents are really angry with me, and some of my really good, straight friends would never take me back now." The fear of failure that the kid was trying to escape in the first place becomes the ultimate self-fulfilling prophecy. Indeed, now it's not paranoia; the user's life really is starting to fall apart. On the other hand, Stage Three users are now so dependent on the drugs that they feel they could not stop even if they wanted to.

A panicky fear sets in, and the teenager looks around for new drugs, new solutions. Even drugs may fail the youth at this stage—tolerance has made them less effective. It is at this point that the kid might get into heavy use of LSD or cocaine. It may also be at this stage that he or she breaks the barrier and goes into intravenous drug use, where the effects are almost instantaneous. It is not unusual in Stage Three to begin to see problems with overdose, drunk-driving citations, or automobile accidents. Stage Three drug abusers may still be hard to detect because they will be holding on in panic to their drug use. They are so invested in it by now that getting out of it is extremely difficult, at best. They have lied so much by this time and typically have gotten so far into stealing and dealing that they feel there would be no way to explain to their parents. As one such kid expressed it, "I made my bed. I knew I had to lie in it." As the pace of the spiral picks up, the teen enters Stage Four of the disease.

Stage Four: Disintegration

At this stage, everything in the drug abuser's life begins to fall apart. School deteriorates, the peer system deteriorates, the family situation deteriorates, and many times the kid gets into serious trouble with the law. By now drug abusers know that they are in real trouble, but they are so invested in their life-style and so hooked on the drugs that they have no hope of coming out of it without outside intervention. They are completely preoccupied with drug use, and they will use repeatedly throughout the day. They get up in the morning and smoke pot in the shower. They stash drugs in various locations for easy access. They may be gone from home for days on end. Most of the time when teenagers don't return home at night, it is because they have overused drugs the night before. They are so stoned or drunk that they know to go home would mean immediate detection. Consequently, they drag their feet and either don't come home at all or wait until a day or two later when they can adamantly deny any accusations of drug use. They feel that it would be much easier to field the punishment for staying out all night than to deal with their parents' having absolute proof that they have been using.

At Stage Four most drug abusers are so preoccupied with their use that they become much more careless about it. They will not work as hard at disguising their using and may even leave paraphernalia lying around the house.

Such blatant and open use could be construed as an angry defiance, an "I don't care" attitude, or it could be a desperate cry for help from a kid whose life is totally out of control. Most of the time it is a mixture of both. Drug users have lost their ability to choose at this point; they have no free agency left. Something must be done by people who care about them before Stage Four reaches its inevitable conclusion: death.

As Stage Four progresses, drug users seldom feel any euphoria. The failure in their lives and the guilt they feel keep them overwhelmed with their pain. They have to use drugs just to bring themselves back up to where they feel normal.

The other factor that makes Stage Four so serious is that any time the kids stop using the drugs, they will go into withdrawal. No matter what drug is involved, there will be a withdrawal syndrome. As soon as the body begins to clear the drug out of the user's system, the kid will drop into a depressed condition in which he or she will feel tremendous psychological pain. To keep that pain from coming about, the drug user must turn back to the drug itself. With increased use, the tolerance builds, and the drugs must be increased again. As the tolerance level grows, it will come closer and closer to the toxic level. The toxic level is the point at which the body can no longer absorb the drug and goes into an overdose condition. The possibility of the drug user's experiencing an overdose becomes more and more certain at this stage. The drug user knows that continued use is a matter of life and death and will knock down anyone or anything that blocks his or her access to drugs.

The progression of the drug-abuse disease is very predictable. Almost all chemically dependent adolescents follow the same sequence. Moving from Stage One to Stage Four usually takes from six to eighteen months. If there are genetic predispositional factors, however, the progression can take place in a matter of weeks. Another factor that can speed the progression of the disease is the age of first use. The younger an adolescent gets into drug use, the more likely it is that he or she will become chemically dependent. Many times a child who is eleven or twelve will be set up to go through the stages very quickly but does not have access to the continual supply or to the amount of money needed to supply the habit. In treatment, however, it is not unusual to find twelve-year-olds who are at Stage Three or even at Stage Four of the disease. The real danger here is that if a child has progressed to that point by age twelve, he or she has very little chance of making it to age eighteen without the disease running its full course. In other words, that child will need significant intervention to keep from dying from the disease.

Another factor that can speed the progression of the disease is the drug of choice. If adolescents pick marijuana, a slow-acting drug, as their drug of choice, the chances are more likely that the disease will take the full eighteen months to reach Stage Four. But if the drug of choice is a fast-acting one such as cocaine, the disease can run its full course in a matter of a few weeks.

We all know that the sooner cancer is detected, the greater the chances are of curing it. Yet many of us fail to go in for appropriate tests and cancer screens. We don't want to believe we might have the problem.

The disease of chemical dependency works the same way. If we could catch a child in Stage One or even Stage Two, we would have a much better chance of curing that child quickly and completely. But we usually don't realize what's going on until the kid is so ill that only drastic measures can save him or her. Parents, being human, fall into two traps that tend to escalate rather than help the disease of chemical dependency. These are called enabling and denial.

Enabling

Enabling is anything a parent does that helps to accelerate the child's deterioration through the disease. Your job as a parent is to prepare your child to become an independent, functioning adult. Anything you do to protect and shelter a child from the consequences and realities of the adult world will become enabling. As one parent said, "I thought I was loving my child when I would bail him out of a jam. Now I realize that he was always counting on me to rescue him. I was encouraging him to keep getting worse."

Most enabling is based on fear. The fear is usually that our children will do something that would reflect negatively on us as parents. If a child exhibits behaviors not in keeping with our value system, we feel we have failed as parents. So we try to cover up for the kid. We make excuses, pay the damages, and get the child out of a jam. The more we rescue our children from suffering the consequences of their behavior, the more they will expect us to bail them out of all their troubles.

Preparing for adulthood is much like preparing for a sporting event. You must exercise and stretch muscles to make them strong enough to withstand the rigors of competition. The same thing is true for our children in getting ready for the competition of the adult world. We must be like coaches and require the discipline that it will take for those children to be ready for the game.

When it comes to getting tough, many of us turn into marshmallows. We have a hard time letting our children hurt. By the time they are teenagers, we should understand the inevitability of pain and the need for it in the process of their growing up; however, as we get older and they get bigger physically, many of us realize that our physical intimidation will not work anymore as a consequence, and we choose to back down from their intimidation. This is a very serious form of enabling. It allows our children to be in control of the family. It also gives them a false sense of freedom. They learn that they don't have to perform inside the rules of any structure. Psychological tests have shown that most of our drug-abusing clients have a distinct problem with being able to function in a structured environment. They are defiant and rebellious against authority and unwilling to comply with any restrictions. This attitude will become very dysfunctional for them in school and in the job market.

To stop the enabling process, you must be unwilling to support your child in behaving in a way that will lead to that child's failure. Of course, children have free agency and also constitutional rights. You can't "make" them behave. But you do have a choice about whether a child will continue to live with you or not. If a kid becomes increasingly incorrigible, there are a number of legal remedies as well as many private resources that can be used to remove that child from your family situation. This point is where the enabling parent becomes very identifiable. Many moms and dads feel as if they have an obligation to provide a home and three meals a day for their child as long as that child needs them. I know of one very caring mother who took the stance, "I vowed to myself as a mother that I would never turn my children away from their home." Consequently, her twenty-two-year-old child was living in her basement, dealing twenty thousand dollars worth of drugs per month. It wasn't until the police surrounded the house one day and arrested several members of the family that she realized she might have been enabling him. Your children will do the same thing. They will take advantage of you as long as you allow them to.

Denial

Denial can be described as any action a parent takes to rationalize, minimize, or avoid the fact that a problem exists. This denial is often seen in the medical field with other forms of childhood diseases. Parents who think their child might have cancer, for instance, will often go to great lengths to deny the existence of the disease. It is almost always a reflection of the parents' inability to handle the fear of what the disease might do to them personally. This problem, like parents' enabling, can often be disguised as loving behaviors toward the child. The parent might become protective or permissive. Denial can also take the form of aggressive and angry behavior, often directed toward people who identify the problem in the child. Many a school administrator has been threatened with lawsuits and personal retaliation by parents who have been informed that their child has a drug problem. Parents also direct their anger at counselors, clergy, neighbors, or even members of their own family. In most families with a teenager who is chemically dependent, at least one parent will be in serious denial. It is easy for the parents to polarize: one becomes the identifier, the other the denier. As one becomes more and more sure that their child has a drug problem, the other will become more and more sure that the first parent is paranoid.

Most of us are able eventually to accept new, painful information, but it takes some of us longer than it takes others. There is an old advertising rule of thumb that people must be exposed to an idea five to seven times before they assimilate it. That rule is true with most parents: they have to be confronted with their child's chemical dependency several times before they begin to accept the fact and stop denying. The real danger in this is that for every month a child's drug use is allowed to continue, the disease will predictably escalate. If your child had cancer and you denied it for several months, you would decrease his or her chances of recovery. Similarly, if you wait to move on your child's chemical dependency, that child's chance of recovering from the disease will deteriorate each month you delay seeking intervention. Sadly, for many parents it takes a crisis like Philip's to bring them out of denial so they will act on the problem.

The next chapter will discuss some typical symptoms of adolescent drug abuse. If you see any of these behaviors, don't close your eyes and take a chance of letting the disease progress. Get the facts, and get help. If you were wrong and your kid really didn't have a problem, you could all have a good laugh over it. Wouldn't it be better to be safe than sorry?

Chapter 4

SYMPTOMS

"Should we arrest your son at school, or should we send the police to your home?" Allison Morris recalls the school principal's words. Eric had been picked up for possession of marijuana. "I protested. I thought there was some mistake, but I told them to do it at school," she says.

When they reached the school, Don and Allison learned that a teacher had seen their son outside with the "rowdy" boys. The teacher wondered, in the first place, why they would be going outside in a blizzard. When he looked out the window and saw Eric's hand reach into a bush, his suspicions became even greater.

The teacher asked Eric what was in his hand, so Eric produced a plastic sandwich bag from the bush. Not good enough. Eric hemmed and hawed with no acceptable response and finally revealed a marijuana joint. But still trying to weasel out, Eric asked, "You didn't see me come out here with those boys, did you?" The teacher thought, and answered no. He also knew that it wasn't the norm for Eric to hang around with them. The negotiations continued, concluding with the story that Eric had innocently gone outside, had been asked to hold the joint for the boys, had been spotted by a teacher, had tried to hide the evidence while the other boys ran—and he was the one to get caught.

"With no doubt in our minds we accepted the story," Allison admits. "But we still felt, as the school did, that it was our duty to enforce some form of punishment."

The school suspended Eric for two days, making it clear that they were enforcing this procedure simply to make sure the students knew that under any circumstances, possession of marijuana meant suspension. Allison and Don also made it clear to Eric that he was being grounded for his behavior simply so the neighbors would know the Morrises had taken this seriously.

"But Don did have a good talk with our son," Allison explains. "He gently, but firmly, told Eric he had made some poor choices today that could affect him for the rest of his life. Eric didn't say a word. He just listened. And the next day he lay on the couch with his head down all day. I felt bad for him. But I knew he needed to think. Hard. And learn a lesson, even if it wasn't his fault."

And indeed Eric was thinking hard but not in quite the way Allison intended. "I just kept going over all the things I should have done so I wouldn't get caught," admits Eric. "I was sulking because I was thinking how stupid I was not to run or something."

Were Don and Allison Morris naive or blind? Or were they just normal parents who, like the rest of us, thought they knew their own son well enough to tell if he would smoke pot or lie about it? We parents like to think we know our children pretty well. It may be hard for us to realize they could use drugs for some length of time without our finding out about it. Does it surprise you to know that the average drug-abusing teenager carries on his activities right under his parents' noses for one and a half to two years?

We can't discount the hidden nature of the disease of drug abuse; however, 80 percent of all chemically dependent youth will follow the same path. The symptoms discussed in this chapter will describe the most typical signs to watch for, but parents should keep in mind that 20 percent of chemically dependent youth will be able to avoid a number of the symptoms described here.

As you read the symptoms that follow, you may want to say, "All kids do that. That's not druggie behavior; that's teenage behavior." Rebellion is a typical example—we expect a certain amount of it from adolescents. The question is, Can we really excuse unacceptable actions on the grounds that everyone is doing them? Chemical dependency is fast becoming typical teenage behavior; can we therefore ignore it as just a phase and hope our child will grow out of it? The answer is obvious: the family needs to take a clear, firm stance in every circumstance but particularly when these symptoms occur. Even a child who is not on drugs will benefit from such a plan of action.

Downward Shift in Peers

One of the most influential changes in an adolescent's life is a change in peer system. Usually, a kid who is getting involved with drugs will at the same time be getting involved with a lower quality of friends. That can happen in one of two ways: either the group that the child grew up in begins to change as a whole or, even more devastating, the child will completely change peer systems. A change in peers is not necessarily bad. It depends on whether you consider such a move to be a deterioration.

A question that I will always ask in a first interview is, "What kind of kids do you hang around with? If I were to ask people at your school what group you belong to, what would they tell me? Does the group that you hang around with have a particular nickname?" Most kids in treatment will be associated with groups called Stoners, Rockers, Punkers, or Partyers. A good portion of the kids will begin to wear paraphernalia that identify them as part of a particular subgroup, including concert T-shirts, long hair, earrings, and tattoos.

But drug abuse cuts across all spectrums. Not all kids will advertise their drug use. Allison says, "I remember being pleased that one of Eric's friends was a student officer, a smart kid. Now I know that this boy, whom my PTA advisers and I had applaudingly reviewed as fit for his office, was really on drugs."

With someone who appears to be more middle-of-the-road and clean-cut a more revealing question might be, "How many of your friends would you consider to be partyers?" or, "Of all your friends, how many are straight, or drug free?" This question often hits home with the clean-cut, churchgoing, middle-class, chemically dependent youth. Many of them will try to maintain a few straight friends just for the sake of appearances. In the later stages of the disease, however, most users throw caution to the wind, and most of their straight friends abandon them.

Parents are often surprised that a child could have been using alcohol and drugs so much without their being aware of it. A peer group working together can be very difficult to catch. They will generally rotate through each other's homes, picking times when the parents are most likely to be gone. This, of course, is easier in a family in which the parents are gone a great deal or have become complacent about the problem. But even in the best of homes it's not unusual to find parties being held downstairs in the basement or upstairs in a bedroom while the rest of the family gathers unawares in another part of the house. Take the case of Natalie, a thirteen-year-old with shining braces that accent a beautiful, innocent smile. Natalie is a druggie. "I would hold parties in the upstairs while my parents were down in the living room," she says. "We had to be fairly quiet, but we got away with it many times."

While we sit at home isolating ourselves from our neighbors, our kids are together, networking with each other and learning from each other's experiences. A tremendous amount of information is exchanged within these relationships.

The peer group is also the main source for drugs and alcohol; a close-knit group will be able to supply each other constantly. They live quite a communal existence; if some members are short of money one week, the rest of the group will always be willing to carry them until they can score some drugs on their own to share around.

The peer group eventually becomes like a very close-knit family or cult group, developing a leadership system and a rigid set of norms and rules. Depending on the leadership that is established, the group can become either quite long-term and stable or very volatile and fickle. In some groups, expectations for membership get higher and higher and the consequences for leaving the group get more and more serious. The kids move rapidly from helping each other deceive their families to breaking the law together.

As the group gets more and more committed to a rebellious and delinquent life-style, the secrets and the confidences can become overpowering. If members begin to feel remorse and try to go back to their old straight life-styles, tremendous pressure can be exerted on them through the fear and anger of the other group members. I have seen this pattern take place among church youth groups, with brothers and sisters, among football team members, and within a group of school officers.

This pattern is not unique to low-income, minority gangs. It is not unusual for middle-class youth who are brought into our treatment facility to have threats come back from their previous peer groups. We hear accusations of brainwashing or communism and threats to break the person out of drug rehabilitation. These threats often come from "good kids" who have gotten way over their heads into something that they are desperately afraid their parents will find out about. They will go to any extreme to try to preserve their life-style.

These defensive acts often produce some of the most tragic consequences of addiction. It is not unusual for our youth coming out of treatment and going back into the public school system to be threatened with physical violence. Anytime a kid is busted at school for a drug-related offense, invariably the other druggies will accuse the recovering youth of "narc-ing,"or turning the drug user in.

Most of our treatment center graduates who go back into school are offered drugs three or four times a day by their old peer group. The peer group has no sympathy for the recovering teenager who has stopped using and is attempting to stay drug free. Instead, the remaining group members usually feel so threatened by the old member who has left and gotten straight that they would do anything they could to bring that person back down to their level. Many recovering kids succumb to the pressure again and slip back into their old, addicted life-styles.

There are two rules about peers in our program: One, if a kid goes back to old friends who use, the kid will use, every single time. Two, if your child's friends are users, your child is a user.

Deterioration in School Performance

"I heard that report cards were out on Friday," says Allison. "But when I asked Eric for it Monday, he said they weren't ready yet. Of course, I believed him." She rolls her eyes as she qualifies her statement. "You know, you could tell when Eric was lying. I used to say his nostrils got big. By gosh, if he told me the grass was purple, I'd probably look twice and get my eyes checked.

"So, anyway, Tuesday I got the report card," she continues. "But I also got a call from Don that the real one was found on his copier at work—with the grades whited out and typed over."

Giving Eric an opportunity to confess and praying that he would, that evening Don and Allison asked their son if a mistake had been made on his report card. To their disappointment, he said no. And to their greater disappointment, when Don slammed the tampered report card down on the table, Eric still denied it. "For twenty minutes he tried to tell us why he wasn't at fault. But we didn't cave in, so he finally admitted the truth. It was then that the possibility of drugs at least crossed my mind," says Don. "Anyway, we knew we had a problem."

It is extremely difficult for a person under the influence of alcohol or drugs to maintain good grades in school. Alcohol is a very fast-acting, intense drug whose effects are difficult to conceal at school. Consequently, most kids will use pot during school hours. In contrast to alcohol, pot is a slow-acting, tranquilizing drug. And the pot our kids smoke today is ten to twenty times stronger than what was available in the early seventies, so a person can get high throughout the day on just a small amount.

The effects of marijuana can easily be disguised from teachers and parents. Most of the kids in our treatment program are smoking pot two or three times a day and then drinking on the weekends to the point of being drunk two or three times a week. This drug-use style can easily be hidden from parents for several months, but over a period of time it begins to take its toll.

Most adolescents will be able to maintain themselves

with occasional drug or alcohol use over a period of several months; however, when they begin to use daily—as so many will—their school performance starts to slide. Usually over a period of three to six months the child will show an increase in tardies and absences. Along with that goes a deterioration in grades. Many parents do not detect this trend and are not notified by school authorities until the student has severely marred his or her grades for that quarter or semester.

When confronted, adolescents will usually talk about how lousy the teachers are and how a number of them are out to get the students for various reasons. They will speak of boredom and the irrelevance of high school classes and will try to convince you in any way they can that the problem is in the educational system and not in them. They will at this point agree to make major changes in their life-style to "really get it together for this semester." If the adolescent is using regularly, this commitment will be virtually impossible to keep, no matter how motivated the kid may seem.

Marijuana creates a distinct apathy syndrome. One of the reasons for this apathy is that marijuana has dramatic effects on a person's short-term memory. Often regular marijuana users will find themselves unable to remember things that they have just read or heard. This effect manifests itself in a number of reading problems. Marijuana users read page 1 of the assignment, and by the time they start reading page 2, they have forgotten what the chapter was about. They find themselves going back over and over the material many times and yet are still unable to retain the information for the test.

The kid on drugs will soon become discouraged and begin not to care about anything. It takes a few months for that attitude to develop, and usually the first areas to suffer are those in which there are specific, measurable expectations. School, then, becomes the first stumbling block in a series of tumbles that the adolescent will take into chemical dependency.

Remember that there are exceptions to the rule. We still have 10 to 20 percent of our kids in treatment who are able to maintain a 3.0 or higher grade point average. We even have a few who have been able to maintain 3.5 to 3.7 grade point averages, even with daily drug use. Trent, for example, who is seventeen, is a good athlete, and he maintains a 3.6 grade point average. He's active in church, and he has carried a tremendous amount of leadership in the family since his dad died a couple of years ago. But Trent is a druggie. When he came into treatment, he was using daily. He was able to maintain his grades, but he was starting to decline in most other areas of his life. Given a bit more time, his grades would have started to come down as well.

Even if a child's grades haven't started to suffer yet, you might notice an increase in tardies and absences. These should serve as red flags and may be early symptoms of drug abuse.

Deterioration of Family Relationships

As a child gets more and more involved in drugs and alcohol, deception starts playing an active role in his or her family life. Drug users must learn how to become expert liars. It's difficult, particularly for a trusting soul like a parent, to believe that our children could lie to us that much. But there is no way that a child could be involved in alcohol and drugs without becoming a very proficient liar.

So the kid begins to break the family rules, confrontations increase, and conflict skyrockets in the family. Arguments over chores, curfew, and independence become a daily event. In just a few short, tragic weeks a harmonious family can jump into chaos and anarchy. (The specific patterns are covered in chapter 9 on family dynamics.) At this point, suffice it to say that the family is becoming more and more stressed and that there will be more and more conflict. This conflict is often demonstrated by verbal and at times even physical abuse of parents by the teenager. Roles seem to polarize as the child increasingly rebels against any wishes of the parent.

As one teenager described it, "I got to where I didn't care about anything or anybody. I would stay out late or not come home at all, just to hide my drug use. I figured I could lie my way out of it the next day and that would be better than getting home on time but getting caught drunk. I soon learned that the best defense was a good offense. If I attacked them, it would get them defensive and distract them from the subject, my drug use. Another thing that I would do is cop (admit) to a smaller problem. I would admit to going to a concert or something that I wasn't supposed to, to cover up that I had really been over at a friend's getting high. Whatever I did, I had to keep my parents off guard to be able to keep on using, and that meant I had to lie all the time."

Parents often feel that the more they try to intervene, the more the child will rebel. You might be tempted at this point, for the sake of peace in the family, to stop trying to intervene. That is a typical enabling behavior. With this progressive, fatal disease, even though the outward situation may become calmer for a while, your adolescent will still be moving deeper and deeper into chemical dependency. The decision to "just let things lie for a while" will be one that you will regret for a long time to come.

Increased Involvement with the Law

For many kids, increasing involvement with the law will go hand in hand with the symptoms that are described above. By definition, a child using alcohol and drugs is involved in illegal activity. Once the kid is thus initiated into the realm of law breaking, he or she more easily justifies other forms of illegal activity.

Few chemically dependent youth would consider themselves to be dealers. When asked if they have ever acted as a go-between, however, they will invariably confirm that they have bought drugs for someone else but didn't receive any money for the service. The fact that they receive a portion of the drugs as payment doesn't seem to count as dealing, in their thinking. It is virtually impossible for a teenager to maintain any kind of a drug habit without getting into some level of dealing. Stealing and shoplifting also become a very common occurrence.

As the disease progresses, it becomes increasingly difficult for kids to hide their intoxicated behavior in public. Their legal entanglements will usually start with curfew violations and truancy, leading next to shoplifting and vandalism, then to public intoxication and possession, and ultimately to burglary, assault, and driving under the influence. Any run-in with the law should serve as a red flag to parents, but any bust for alcohol- or drug-related offenses should serve as three to five red flags.

Kids are like adults. They seldom get caught red-handed doing something wrong. For example, many estimates suggest that an adult driving under the influence has only one chance in 250 of being picked up. The same is true for adolescents. If they get picked up once for an alcohol or drug offense, the chances are extremely high that they are already chemically dependent. If they get picked up twice or more, it is almost certain.

Changes in Personal Habits

To be able to fit in with their peer group and to symbolize the rebellion in their lives, many drug users will significantly change their appearance. They will begin to advertise their newfound life-style by dressing in clothes that promote the drug/rock culture. These kids are usually pretty easy to spot; however, some less dramatic changes in personal habits and appearance are designed specifically to cover up drug and alcohol use. Often teens will change clothes several times a day to disguise the odor of marijuana smoke. Sometimes a kid will wear a coat all day and then remove it as he walks in the door; or he'll leave the coat off while he's smoking pot and then put it on to disguise the odor when he gets home.

Another typical behavior change is for kids to become increasingly territorial about their rooms. They don't want you coming in to clean or pick anything up, and in many cases they will put locks on their doors to keep everyone out.

Marked mood swings can be a danger signal. Teenagers often go from being quite lethargic to seeming suddenly filled with pent-up energy. If you notice that this type of mood shift is associated with trips to the basement or bathroom, you need to raise the question of stimulant drugs.

Something else to watch for is a teen's tendency to experience more and more swings into serious depression, accompanied by marked changes in sleeping and eating patterns. Treat this mood very seriously. More and more teenagers are committing suicide, and it is important for parents to ask if the teenager has ever thought about taking his or her own life or is now thinking about it.

When drugs are associated with the depression, there will typically be some rhythmic pattern to it. An hour after coming home, the teenager drops off into a deep and heavy sleep, a sleep from which he or she can't be awakened. The teen's bedtime will change, and he or she will start getting up later and later in the morning.

Another typical mood swing is for a teenager to become more and more volatile. Even a youth with no history of temper outbursts or aggression can over a period of a few weeks become very aggressive, both verbally and physically, when using drugs. Any continuing series of mood swings calls for investigation and intervention.

Evidence of Drug Use—The Surest Indicator

Finally, the most important indicator of drug abuse is actual evidence of intoxication or drug use. As mentioned earlier, the average length of time between when a teenager starts using drugs regularly and when his parents are able to catch him red-handed is eighteen months to two years. By the time you start seeing suspicious actions or finding items of drug paraphernalia, the problem has most likely progressed into the later stages of chemical dependency.

Often when on speaking engagements, our kids at Dayspring will describe how they hid their use from their parents: "I'd smoke marijuana in the shower every morning before I'd go to school. I hid the pipe in the space behind a picture frame in the bathroom. I hid the pot inside the rod in my closet." "I would hide my stash anywhere I thought my parents would never look: inside speakers, in the ceiling, under my mattress, and even in their room. You find that drawer in your parents' chest that nobody's been in for years. They never found it there." "I would change my clothes three or four times a day to hide the smell. We usually smoked pot outside, or if we were in a car, we'd roll down the windows." "I always wore a lot of cologne or hair spray to cover up the smell. I always had a bottle of Visine with me to take the red out of my eyes. I also wore sunglasses a lot." "I would make sure I looked stoned all the time whether I was or not. That way no one would see the difference. I would make sure I got stoned just before going to a new job or class, just so the people there would think that was the way I always was." "I would always make curfew so my parents wouldn't get suspicious. I kept my hair short and wore preppy clothes so that I could deal without marking myself as a druggie. I carried Binaca with me all the time so I could kiss my mom good night and she wouldn't smell anything. If she did I just said it was someone else or would admit to having had a puff on someone's cigarette."

Our kids are such experts at being able to hide their use that it's only when they get heavily entrenched in the apathy syndrome that they become careless and detectible in their use. For many this carelessness is a secret cry for help.

There are several typical scenarios that describe how parents are made aware that their child is using drugs. One scenario is a confrontation at school. Many times a teacher or administrator will call the parents and say that they suspect drug use. But since most teachers and administrators are so tired of being threatened with lawsuits and of listening to irrational parents defend their children, many of them have just stopped calling unless there is harder evidence. Don't ever ignore this kind of call—remember, these people see your kids in a completely different context from the one you see them in.

Another scenario for detection is an adolescent being caught in possession of alcohol or drugs. Frequently the parents are notified, and the teenager offers the old line, "Mom, I swear to you it isn't mine. I was just holding it for a friend." In all the years that I have counseled chemically dependent teenagers, I can't remember one time when it proved to be true that the teenager was actually holding drugs for someone else. Most teenagers would never give their drug stash to anyone else. And no one would be dumb enough to take someone else's drugs, for fear of being caught with them.

The first time a teenager is confronted with hard evidence, a sincere and pleading defense will usually throw the parents off the track. They will hope—they want desperately to believe—that it was just a terrible mistake and that their child was just too naive and should have known better than to hold someone else's drugs. If you fall for that old line without seriously investigating the possibility that your child has a drug problem, you may be allowing a fatal disease to continue to progress in that child. Liken this to finding some abnormal growth on your child's body and rationalizing that it just isn't worth taking the child to the doctor. If it were cancer and you waited another six months before doing anything about it, your complacency could cost your child's life. The same is true with drug and alcohol abuse. It is your job as a parent to investigate any kind of activity that could jeopardize your child's life. If you have to come to the point that your children think you are paranoid, so be it.

When the police pick up a child for a drug-related offense, it is not unusual for them to say that they are very busy and cannot take a lot of time to process juvenile possession charges. They will probably give you a call and either have the child dropped off or have you come down to pick up the child. If you have hit them on a good day, your child might get a fatherly lecture from some police officer. That is often the extent of any involvement by legal authorities. Anytime a child is picked up for drug or alcohol possession or for a public intoxication charge, you should have a thorough, professional evaluation done on that child to see if he or she is chemically dependent. Remember, the chances are very slim that kids are going to get picked up the first or even the fiftieth time that they are intoxicated.

Even more serious are such charges as burglary, theft, vandalism, DUI, or assault in which alcohol and drugs are suspected as a motive or part of the crime. Such an arrest indicates that the adolescent has a significant drug problem and has had to resort to more serious crimes to be able to maintain it. A DUI (driving under the influence of alcohol) or DWI (driving while intoxicated) should always be seen as a very serious offense and as a major violation of family rules. Anytime a child is picked up in a car in which someone is intoxicated, whether driving or not, he is moving a lethal weapon toward an unknowing public. This offense should warrant at least a thorough evaluation and probably an automatic admission into some kind of treatment.

Still another typical scenario is that you will find a plastic bag filled with an oregano-like substance, strange-looking little round seeds, or some kind of white powder. If you ever find a plastic sandwich bag containing an unknown substance, take it to a police station or a hospital to be analyzed. Also, many times parents will stumble across some kind of drug paraphernalia. Small metal or wooden or glass pipes, alligator clips that are used as roach clips, cigarette rolling papers, tiny weight scales, larger water pipes, or any kind of unknown substance in suspicious containers should all be processed through local law enforcement authorities or drug treatment centers to identify what kind of substance or paraphernalia it is. Confirmed identification of drug paraphernalia should serve as a major warning sign of regular drug abuse. If you find such things in your house or car, you need to look toward some serious type of intervention that would restrict your child and help you determine whether he or she is chemically dependent.

One of the best technologies available to us today is urinalysis. Many laboratories, hospitals, and doctors' offices can analyze urine samples for most of the major drugs of abuse. It is best to get a sample as soon as possible after a suspected drug-use episode. A slow-acting drug, such as marijuana, may be detected as much as a week after use, but a faster-acting drug may disappear within a day or two. A typical drug screen takes two to three days to process and will cost between fifteen and thirty dollars. More advanced techniques of mass spectroscopy provide drug-use evidence that is even admissable in court. The confirmation of mass spectroscopy may cost more, but it is well worth it if there are any doubts in the urinalysis.

If your child shows any one of these symptoms, which are summarized in the checklist below, don't ignore it. Don't suppose that your close-knit, loving, religious family is immune. As Allison Morris says, "Never mind that our son looked like one of the straight kids. Never mind that we were leaders in our LDS ward and tried to live according to our religion. Never mind that I was always here for the kids, didn't work outside my home except with the PTA and church, where I could do nice things for and with my kids. Never mind that we lived in a nice home and shared nice times together in it. Just never mind. We've been in the Dayspring program for months now. And I know my little lamb is an addict/alcoholic. The same as the rest of them."

Once you have confirmed that your child is using drugs, evaluation and intervention are the next steps. The intervention process can be very volatile and requires some sound strategy by both parents. The next chapter will show you some proven techniques to increase your chance for positive results with your chemically dependent adolescent.

Is My Kid Using Drugs?
A Checklist of Common Symptoms

Downward Shift in Peers

Lifelong friendships begin to deteriorate.

New, bad friends begin to appear.

The child tends to hide new friendships.

If the child's peers use, the child uses.

Deterioration in School Performance

The child's grades start to drop.

The child has been missing classes more frequently.

The child seems uninterested, apathetic.

Deterioration of Family Relationships

Family conflict increases.

The child violates curfew.

The child is increasingly aggressive with parents.

The child is constantly testing rules.

Increase in Involvement with the Law

Any drug-related charge (possession, public intoxication, driving under the influence) is a sure sign of drug involvement.

The child is picked up for shoplifting, vandalism, or breaking and entering.

Changes in Personal Habits

The child exhibits sudden mood swings.

Eating and sleeping patterns are disturbed.

Personal appearance deteriorates.

The child drops out of church activities.

The child becomes increasingly defiant of any authority.

The child is unusually apathetic.

Evidence of Drug Use—The Surest Indicator

You find drug paraphernalia or plastic sandwich bags containing unknown substances.

You catch your child drunk or stoned.

You receive reports from school of drug use or suspected drug use.

Your child uses a lot of eye drops or cologne or incense to cover up smells.

Your child gets caught with drugs, but says, "I was just holding it for a friend."

Chapter 5

INTERVENTION

Eight o'clock. As usual, music was blasting from Craig's downstairs bedroom. Not so usual was the sensation slithering through his mother's bones. "I just had that feeling," Jeanne Peterson recalls. "So I went downstairs to check it out. He'd made up his room to look like he was there. But he wasn't. I was angry and worried. No, I was mad. He'd done this too many times before. I had told him, 'If you go this time, you're gone. Forever.' But I wondered, did he really understand what I meant?"

A rush of emptiness replaced the tingle from moments before. Jeanne jumped in the car and rushed down to the bus stop. Craig wasn't there. She shoved the accelerator to full force and followed the bus route until she caught up with the bus. Craig was just getting off. "Craig!" Her voice was propelled by the force of this past half hour and a year's worth of half hours just like it. "Craig, listen to me. Listen. If you leave, you're not coming back. I mean it, Craig. You're not coming back. Not ever."

What do you do when your child's life is out of control? If you suspect that drugs and alcohol are involved, the time has come for a process called intervention. *Intervention* is the term used to describe the act of confronting a drug user with the reality of how out of control his or her life is and insisting on a change. Interventions are done by people whom the teen considers to be significant: parents, teachers, clergy, siblings, friends, or anyone else that has seen the deterioration and could have an effect on the teen. Very few teenagers will come forward themselves about their drug problem. At Dayspring we estimate that only about one in twenty admissions comes from a teenager who volunteers for treatment. It is up to the parents to act. They must be the ones to force the situation through an intervention.

Interventions always feel volatile. Teenagers do not like to hear the truth. A teenager in the middle of an intervention will often blow up and storm out of the room. Many parents are afraid that if they push the issue, the teenager will run away from home and ultimately commit suicide. The extreme sensitivity of the confrontation makes it absolutely critical that the parents plan how to conduct the intervention to get the best results.

The process of intervention is very tricky. It is a little like trying to catch a puppy that doesn't want to get caught. Sometimes, the more effort you make, the worse the situation gets; you may chase it right in front of an oncoming car. That is why it is so critical to use the utmost strategy in setting up your intervention.

Another good way to describe the process of intervention comes from experiences I had on the farm in Kansas where I spent many of my summers. We often had to bring the cattle down into the corral. They always had a pretty good idea that when we headed them for the corral it was to poke them, brand them, inject them, or do some other painful thing to them. Consequently, a number of them would get quite resistant.

The strategy of moving the cattle toward the gate was well thought out beforehand. It was imperative to have all the hands evenly spaced in a circle to be able to head off any end runs that might occur. The closer we got to the gate, the more likely it was that things would become volatile. When the time came to actually force the cattle through the gate, each participant had to stay on his toes to shut off all avenues of escape. Even then, it wasn't unusual to come to a face-to-face confrontation with an unusually resistant steer. Many times it boiled down to a fifty-fifty proposition about whether we would actually get that resistant one in the corral. It was a fine art, and I greatly respected my uncle, who seldom lost a battle with those steers.

Like corralling cattle, intervention is a great art.

Sometimes you win, sometimes you lose—but there are strategies you can use to increase your chances of actually getting that steer into the corral, that is, getting your child into treatment.

The Setting and the Participants

Most interventions take place after some crisis has occurred in a teenager's life. Maybe the teenager has been busted for possession or driving under the influence, or the parents have found the teenager drunk or stoned or with paraphernalia. A crisis might come after a school quarter has ended when the parent finds a number of failing grades or after a urine test has come back with positive results.

The setting for an intervention is most often in a professional's office. That is because parents will frequently offer the ultimatum: "Either you will go in to see a counselor with us, or you will no longer live in this home." The intervention could also take place at the young person's home, but it is helpful to have an outside mediator to referee the proceedings. Regardless of the setting, it is important that the time be absolutely uninterrupted. There should be only enough chairs for the participants, and those chairs should be in a circle close to each other and all facing one another.

All participants should be selected beforehand and briefed on their parts in the intervention. Each participant should write down how the teenager's druggie life-style has affected his or her life. It is imperative that the participants talk about their feelings and not lecture the teenager. They need to move through their presentations quickly and clearly, emphasizing the feelings that they are having. The presentation should be as loving and calm as possible, but it must be absolutely honest.

If a counselor is not present, one person should be designated as the leader of the intervention. All participants should be assembled beforehand and have an idea of what the order of presentation will be. It is critical that all participants support the need for intervention with this teenager. It is not unusual for a using sibling or relative to come to the defense of the teenager in the midst of the intervention process. As the pressure builds, it is quite easy for a participant to suddenly start enabling the chemically dependent teenager by going to his defense. If this happens, it is critical for the leader of the intervention to gently but firmly instruct the enabler to please hold any comments until the leader recognizes the person.

As the pressure builds, so will the teen's desire to get up and leave the room. One small detail that can become critical is where the teen is seated. Arrange the seating beforehand so that the teenager is seated away from any doors. It always helps to have a couple of the more supportive male participants sitting between the teenager and the door. It can also help to start out the intervention with a brief statement to the effect that "the things you hear may be painful and hard to accept, but if you want to remain a part of this family, you must stay in this room until we are all finished." The reason for all the precautions is that if the teenager does bolt and leave the room, it may be impossible to muster the participants with the necessary energy for another intervention.

If you are confident that your teenager is going to require treatment, it is even more essential to have the intervention occur on the premises of the treatment facility. That makes it much easier to escort the reluctant teenager to the treatment unit immediately.

Cory, who is now a graduate of our program, reflects on his first visit to Dayspring: "I can remember being in the intake session with my parents. It wasn't until twenty minutes into the interview that the words *drug rehab* came up. Boy, was I mad. If looks could kill, my mom would be dead. I hated the counselor and my parents really bad at that point. It took a few days before I began to realize how much I had needed that to happen. Now I look at it as one of the best things that ever happened to me." That is a response I have heard countless times as recovering teens have reflected on their interventions.

The intervention process is much like taking a child to a doctor or a dentist for some treatment that you know will be painful. The child can't really understand the need to be punctured by a doctor's needle or to have teeth drilled by a dentist. Similarly, the chemically dependent teenager may feel betrayed and hurt, but you as a parent know that the brief pain of intervention is worth a confrontation when the alternative is the long-term pain of letting the disease progress. It is a parent's responsibility to make sure that a teenager is forced to face these realities.

If you had a diabetic child who was not caring for himself properly or taking the appropriate medication, you would do whatever it took to make that child confront the reality of his choices—no matter how painful that reality might be. The drug user who chooses the adult path and leaves home assumes the responsibility of deciding whether to care for himself or herself or to deteriorate in the disease. Until that time, however, it is the parents' job to be sure the child knows the consequences of the choice to abuse drugs.

The Process of the Intervention

After the plan has been formulated, the participants have been lined up, and the location has been prepared, you are ready to inform the teenager of the upcoming meeting. The timing can be critical. The idea is to do whatever you think gives you the highest chance of actually getting that teenager into that room. What that is depends on your relationship and on how volatile the teen is. The best case, if the kid will accept it, is to explain that you are going to a counselor at a drug treatment facility to evaluate the child's need for treatment. That is usually done a short time before actually leaving for the intervention, but in the best cases it can be done the evening before. You would seldom tell the teen more than one day before the meeting, however. The reason for this is that the more teenagers think about going to a drug treatment facility, the more their imaginations run wild. They visualize brainwashing sessions and prison bars.

Since the intervention is usually brought on by some kind of crisis, it is best to schedule the intervention one or at most two days after the crisis has occurred. You want to have enough time to orchestrate the intervention while at the same time using the natural lead-in of the crisis.

In the worst cases, warning the child of the meeting that is going to take place increases the chances of the child's running away or committing some self-destructive act. It may become necessary just to take the youth forcibly to the intervention. In such cases, it is increasingly important to hold the intervention at a treatment facility rather than in your own home. If the teenager is that volatile, it will likely be too difficult for the parents to try to control him or her at home. If you and your intervention participants are unable to forcibly move the child to the location of the intervention, the only alternative you will have is to use law enforcement officers.

Most law enforcement agencies are unwilling to intervene in a family conflict unless it is set up beforehand. Most will require that there have been some heavy legal involvement before they would feel justified to step in and move the child to a more restrictive environment. When there is legal involvement, judges can be extremely helpful in bringing about the intervention. A court hearing is an excellent time to obtain the leverage needed to move a child into treatment. It is important that you let the court worker know beforehand that you suspect an alcohol and drug problem and would like for this child to be evaluated. It is also important to let the worker know whether you can afford to pay for a treatment center yourself or whether you would need to rely on a state-funded agency. Most judges are very cooperative in mandating a treatment facility when there is evidence of the need, especially if the parents are willing to pick up the bill.

Another important consideration is that the child does have civil rights. This legality can complicate the process of intervention a great deal. In most states, as soon as a child turns sixteen, he or she has the right to refuse treatment. The kid could legally choose to walk out of a program. That puts you as a parent in a double bind. You are legally responsible for the child, and yet you cannot put that child into treatment without his or her consent. The only leverage you then have left is whether you allow the child to continue to live with you. Because of the civil rights issue, most treatment programs will refuse to accept a child sixteen or over without that child's consent to be there.

As you carry out the intervention, several other strategic factors should be considered. When the teenager is seated in the room with the rest of the participants, the leader should lay the ground rules and open up the discussion. The atmosphere should be loving and calm, but the participants must be tough and honest about their feelings and about the effect of the drug situation in their lives. Participants should be instructed to talk when they are called upon or to have the leader recognize them if they have something important to say. Again, it should be emphasized to the participants that they should talk about their feelings. The introduction from the first family member, typically the father, could go as follows, "Son, I love you, but I am concerned that I see your life deteriorating in many areas. I have seen problems in the following areas: . . . "

It is important to remind participants to use "I" messages. Rather than continually saying *we* feel this or *we* think that, each participant should personalize the effect the drug use has had on his or her own life. It is also important not to use the word *you* too often. "You" messages can become very accusatory. The teenager can usually hear the information better if it is personalized with "I" messages: for example, "I have great fears about the direction of your life. I am greatly saddened to watch your deterioration. I feel that we are losing our relationship." This is in contrast to such statements as, "You never come home on time. You really make me mad. You are just lazy."

At this point it is important to go through briefly, but with emphasis, the major areas of concern. These usually include deterioration in school, peer relationships, family relationships, personal habits, legal involvements, and especially any hard evidence of drug and alcohol abuse.

Next, the participant should express what his or her greatest fear is if things don't change. At this point the intervention can become quite emotional, and it is critical for the leader to emphasize that the participant talk about feelings. It is usually appropriate for the leader to wait a couple of minutes for the participant to work through those feelings. If the participant cannot continue, however, the leader then sums up what the person was saying and moves on to the next person. It's best during this confrontation part of the intervention to keep each participant's contribution to about three to five minutes. This time frame can vary according to the number of participants involved, but the entire intervention should last somewhere between thirty and forty-five minutes.

The goal of the intervention is to push the teenager to get some kind of outside help. (The various kinds of help available will be discussed in the next chapter.) If during the process of the intervention – perhaps after an especially emotional exchange – the teenager appears ready to seek that treatment, it may be advantageous to end the intervention or limit further discussion. That is why it's important to start the intervention with those people who will have the most effect on the teenager. The leader may want to summarize the remaining presentations but should encourage the participants to go more quickly and with less confrontation. Each participant must at some point during treatment express his or her resentments and concerns and fears, but that may best be done in the first week or two of the treatment program rather than in the intervention. If the teenager does not agree to try treatment, the next critical step is to issue the ultimatum.

The Ultimatum

The ultimatum is the expression of the consequences that the parents feel they will have to carry out if the child chooses not to seek help. It is the bottom line: "Get help, or else." A typical ultimatum might be: "Susie, your mother and I both love you very much, but our job as parents is to help you become an independent, successful adult. If you feel that our parenting is no longer useful for you, and you choose not to seek help for this problem, we feel that we can no longer support you living with us and the rest of the family. We do want you to continue living with us, but you must be a part of the family if you are going to live in our home. That means you must follow our rules and live up to our basic expectations. We both love you and hope you choose to continue to stay with us."

It is important that the ultimatum be delivered in a calm, clear, loving, and firm voice. Here it is more appropriate to use a "we" message, to demonstrate the parents' unity on this decision. The speech should be given by one of the parents, and it is essential that the parents be united on it. If parents haven't discussed the bottom-line ultimatum thoroughly before the intervention and come to absolute agreement, the teenager will manipulate the situation. If the parents become angry or start arguing with each other during the intervention, they will give the teenager an excuse to disqualify anything that they say. The ultimatum must convince the child that if he or she continues the druggie life-style, you will remove that child from the home.

For the ultimatum to work, the parent has to have investigated all alternatives. If the child refuses to cooperate and calls your bluff, you must have chosen consequences that you can carry out. These can include the teenager's being taken to the local youth services center, being sent to an informed relative's house, being put into a more restrictive, lockup type of treatment center, or, in worst cases, being kicked out of the home. The teenager will almost always pick the least restrictive pathway, so it is important that you give only alternatives that you can live with and that meet your minimum requirements. In other words, don't leave a weak link, or the teenager will choose it every time. Unacceptable alternatives include living with an older brother or sister who possibly uses drugs, living with a friend who possibly uses, or going to live with a family member who would be permissive. Once the ultimatum is given, it is important to press for a decision right then and there.

One thing that we have done at Dayspring to streamline this process is to offer the teenager a two-day trial period in our program. This trial period gives us a chance to confirm our evaluation of the situation, and it also gives the teenager a chance to see what drug rehabilitation is really like. Most kids drop their initial fears after the two days. This trial period does not, however, supersede the need for a strong consequence from the parents if the child refuses treatment. Whatever consequence is chosen, you must be ready to carry it out immediately after the intervention.

Strategic Withdrawal, or Street Therapy

The most difficult ultimatum to deliver is to ask the child to leave the home, but if your child refuses all other alternatives and you have no legal recourse, this action may be the only choice. To be able to put yourself back in the driver's seat in your own home, you must have a commitment from that teenager to change his or her lifestyle. The effectiveness of this ultimatum lies in the fact that the child will not appreciate what he or she has until it is gone. Another term for this stance is *strategic withdrawal.* The thought of it turns many parents pale, but if you are not able to take a tough-love position, the child will again assume control of the situation and be the one who is running the family.

I had a good friend, a university professor, who had a very large Labrador retriever named Bo. Every time I went to his house I went to the backyard to see how Bo was doing. Bo was quite a boisterous, energetic dog, and it wasn't unusual to be greeted by two front paws in the middle of the chest. My friend had built a very expensive kennel but never seemed to be able to contain Bo in it. The dog was famous for rampaging the garden and especially for tearing up the prized tomato plants.

Every time I went to my friend's house, Bo seemed to be outside his kennel and to have full rein in the backyard. Finally, one summer I went out back and found Bo in his usual controlling position. My gaze wandered over to the expensive kennel and there, inside the chain link fence, were the tomato plants. Bo had finally won the battle.

Many times I see parents who are cowering in their bathrooms or bedrooms, trying to get some respite from their children. When the children become energetic and aggressive adolescents, it's not unusual for them to control the entire home while parents shiver in the corner, hoping they will leave soon. I use the retriever example as a graphic reminder that we are the builders of the kennel, the architects of the family, and we are the ones who need to be in control of our homes. If we don't take the time and energy to build good rules and to enforce them, we too will find our children in control of our lives. To regain control of our home may mean that we will have to practice strategic withdrawal from one of our teenagers.

Of the chemically dependent kids that I have seen treated successfully, most have had parents who have been willing to go to the wall with them over the issue of control and family stability. In other words, in just about every one of these cases the parents have had to invite the child to either follow the rules or find someplace else to live. This ultimatum is emotionally much easier to give to a seventeen-year-old than to a thirteen-year-old, but the principle still applies. If our fears overrule us and we allow ourselves to be intimidated and to compromise our values, the children will have free rein in whatever they want to do. If we are more restrictive and insist on our teenagers' following the rules, they may "hate" us for a period of time, but usually at the same time they know that they need those restrictions.

The beauty of strategic withdrawal is that if it is done with a heart full of love and with self-control, many times adolescents will change their minds and conform more closely to family standards. In the harder cases the child may actually have to go outside the home for a few days to a few months.

The key to sending the child out of the home is to simulate the kind of life-style that the teenager would be subjected to if he or she were to live independently. It may be best just to put the child out on the street; however, many parents feel an obligation to set their children up in some kind of alternative living arrangement. If you choose this option, make the arrangement an austere one. Estimate the amount of money you would save by having the child out of your house. Compare that to what it would take for him or her to live at current subsistence level. Then take some figure in between. The strategy here is that you want to make the child see how difficult it would be to be self-supporting. The aim is to help that kid understand and appreciate how much you have contributed to the betterment of his or her life. A youth may have to experience the austerity of the street to truly appreciate your contribution.

It is best not to give the teen any more cash than is absolutely necessary because the kid will most often turn around and use extra money to buy drugs. To eliminate the exchange of actual money, you can make a direct rent payment, provide groceries rather than food money, and provide bus passes rather than gas money. A critical factor is to establish a specific amount and never exceed that amount. Chemically dependent teenagers are experts at learning how to manipulate parents. They will find ways to push the guilt button so that parents will increase their contribution. Many parents choose not to support the teen financially at all; that is something that you will have to decide yourself. If you do decide to subsidize the child financially, it is important to pick a specific dollar amount that you can feel comfortable with. And it is important for the teen to understand that that amount in this world will barely allow for survival.

The goal of intervention is to help your teenager admit to the problem and seek some sort of help that you find acceptable. If that doesn't happen, the process may have to be repeated over and over again. Even if the child does agree to seek treatment, it is important for the ultimatum to remain clear and ever present. It needs to become a rule in your household that no one will use drugs illegally and remain a part of the household.

When your suspicions are confirmed about a drug or alcohol problem, the best alternative may lie in treatment. Treatment programs vary a great deal, and it pays to shop around. The next chapter will deal with the question of how to find a good, effective treatment program for your teenager.

CHAPTER 6

TREATMENT

"We spent the years when treatment might have been effective at home denying that we had a problem and telling ourselves that if we made a big deal of it we would create even larger problems. If I had it to do over again, I'd skip the reports from school, and the threats, and go straight to the urine scan. Armed with proof of drug use, I'd get my boys professional treatment," says Vic Earnshaw.

The step into a drug treatment program is a big one. It will be costly in both time and money but not nearly as costly as letting the disease progress. In a day and age when treatment varies a great deal, it's important to shop around. If your child had cancer, you would check out every possible option. You must do the same in looking for the best chemical dependency treatment program.

In this chapter when I refer to treatment, I'm generally not talking about outpatient psychotherapy. Many times this may have been the first step. But if the disease has progressed past Stage Two, once-a-week therapy with a counselor is generally ineffective. Also, many counselors, psychologists, and psychiatrists know nothing about chemical dependency and will waste a lot of time and money on other issues. So we will assume that these approaches have been tried and that you are looking for a more intensive model.

When searching for an expensive product or professional service, people generally rely on the evaluation of friends, acquaintances, and other professionals. Similarly, the best way to find a treatment program is to identify someone you trust who is knowledgeable about the disease of chemical dependency and has some familiarity with programs in your area. This person could be a friend, a professional, or a parent who has experienced this problem in his or her family. You might also call your local government alcohol and drug authorities and ask them to describe the various programs that exist. Identify three to five that you think provide the services that you may be looking for. Then go shopping.

Many will be adult-only treatment programs and can be eliminated. Many others will provide only outpatient therapy once a week or so. That may be a place to start, but a child in the later stages of the disease will be able to con most therapists. You may have to look outside your area to find a chemical dependency treatment program for teenagers; however, it's best to have one within driving distance, so that you can be assured of ongoing support groups. That will be critical in the later stages of treatment.

"We reached a point where we'd say in our prayers at night, 'God, if our son is going to die, please let it be soon.' That was an honest, awful feeling. But Aaron's drug addiction had not only made him sick but it had taken the family down with it. We all needed out," Derrick and Theresa Clayson remember.

Can a treatment program really help your child? The statistics are stark, and parents should have a realistic view from the beginning. The best programs in the country have about a 40 percent recovery rate; many programs have closer to 15 or 20 percent success. But when the alternative to treatment is likely to be death, it is certainly worth a try.

Who can put the pieces together for a family that has eroded slowly through an eight-year battle with a drug-addicted son?

"We didn't even know if it could be done," admits Theresa Clayson. "I was a blithering idiot, spending my days on the phone talking to psychiatrists and counselors at drug rehabilitation programs. Then Derrick took a week off work, and we went frantically from one program to another. First we'd check for price, but no one could give us even a good round figure because it depended on the length of Aaron's stay. Then we'd look at the surroundings and decor, but too often we felt like we were in an insane asylum. Then we'd ask about the treatment program itself, which was usually five weeks to a couple of months, leaving the kid on his own for follow-up. But we'd wonder if he would really follow up. Could a kid who walked around like a zombie, who talked in monotone, who didn't care about anything but drugs—could our Aaron really be changed enough in five weeks to follow up with AA meetings, or whatever else was suggested, on his own?

"A friend suggested Dayspring. They gave us a ballpark cost figure, told us the program would last a minimum of one year, and mentioned family treatment. We were sure Aaron needed to be locked in someplace. Then we caught wind of Aaron's plans to leave for California in two days and knew we just had to do it."

The next day, Theresa and Derrick took Aaron to Dayspring. Aaron decided to stay because of one component the Claysons hadn't thought to look for: peer support. "I walked in and felt like these kids were from my own crowd," he explains.

Within days, Aaron's parents and little sister were beginning their own treatment through parent and family support groups. They were embraced by people who knew what they were feeling and could offer an ear willing to listen and a heart willing to care. Almost two years later, they were challenged to break away to rebuild a normal life on their own. But they are comforted, knowing that their friends through the program will always be just a phone call away.

Treatment Philosophy

Programs vary widely in their approach to chemical dependency. In general, you should look for programs that treat chemical dependency as a disease. There must be acknowledgment that whatever the original cause of the alcohol and drug experimentation, chemical dependency is a primary disease and must be addressed before you can move on to anything else. Many programs take a more psychological approach, viewing chemical dependency as only a symptom of some underlying problem. The danger in that approach is in greatly underestimating the power of the drugs. Ten or fifteen years ago most teenagers seen in drug treatment had serious psychological problems and serious family deterioration. That's not the case today. We see many kids with clean psychological profiles, from strong families. We still get a good number with those underlying problems, but we also see many kids who do not fit any of the predictive patterns. But even kids who do have some psychological impairment must get a hold on the drug problem before they can go on to work on other psychological issues. Most good drug treatment programs will combine the two but will maintain a strong emphasis on total abstinence from alcohol and drugs.

You should visit the treatment center first and talk to the director or the counselors about their philosophies toward drug use and treatment. If they have wishy-washy stances toward a teen's use of marijuana and alcohol, I would advise you not to place your child in that facility.

Look for a structured treatment program. Treating chemically dependent adolescents is a very difficult task. Each child has some individual idiosyncrasies about his or her chemical dependency, but most follow the same general pattern. The most successful programs use a structured approach that requires the adolescent to earn back levels of freedom through fulfilling assignments and tasks. This structure is essential because few adolescents have the cognitive structure of self-discipline to develop their own individualized program.

The program needs to have a strong peer leadership and peer counseling component. There are two reasons for this. First, it is usually much easier for peers to break through a teenager's wall of denial. Second, the kids need to help other kids to strengthen their own programs. We have all learned that the best way to learn something yourself is to have to teach it. Also, when a teenager affects another human being's life for the better, maybe even saves that person, it provides that teenager with a stronger feeling of meaning in life than he or she has typically ever experienced. Lack of meaning in life is one of the main causes of drug abuse. Ironically, many of the kids would never have found this power and meaning had they not sunk so low themselves through their drug problem.

There is no doubt in my mind that our most successful kids keep their own recovery program strong by helping out others who have the same problem. Their peer counseling is paradoxical in that they find themselves in a "parental" role with some young druggie who has the same denial pattern and the same out-of-control behavior that they had. That new young druggie will use the same excuses and the same lines that they used a few months before. By reversing their role in becoming peer counselors, many of them are able to relate much more quickly to what their parents have gone through.

The peer component also allows for all the kids to go through similar requirements and rites of passage. The esprit de corps that develops is essential in maintaining support groups after they get out of treatment. It's helpful if they have a "graduating class" to stay close to after treatment ends. I maintain strongly that in most cases peers got them into drugs and peers will have to get them out.

Few people can deny that the most successful treatment programs in the country are those that use the approach of Alcoholics Anonymous and Narcotics Anonymous. For many years I resisted involvement with that community, probably for the same reasons you have resisted. Generally, we picture a group of craggy old men sitting in a smoke-filled room talking about things that no one else can be involved in. It immediately raises our suspicion. After having been involved for the past few years in this fraternal organization, however, I have been very impressed with what they have been able to accomplish. Most of our successful kids in treatment have become heavily involved in AA and NA.

What these groups provide is a long-term support system that the kids can rely on whenever they begin to struggle. In any city or town there will always be AA and NA meetings. Teenagers can immediately find a group of people with whom they hold common values, people who understand their problems and can identify with how they could be struggling with cravings for drugs and alcohol.

Another important component of AA and NA is the

twelve-step recovery program. The twelve-step model has been used by millions of people to work through major life issues and find new meaning for their lives. Especially for alcoholics and drug addicts, it provides a way of looking at dealing with their problem and finding a new, fresh start.

The twelve-step program takes a spiritual view of life. The twelve steps start out with requiring alcoholics and drug addicts to own their problem and work through recognizing their inability to deal with this problem by themselves. They must identify a higher power, or God, that they can rely on to begin to have faith in their lives again. They must do a searching moral inventory of their lives and share those findings with themselves, God, and one other human being. It is at this point that many alcoholics and addicts find forgiveness for themselves for their past deeds and a freedom that allows them to move on to work on other issues. The twelve-step program ends with a commitment to go on taking the message to other people.

Length of Treatment

Teenagers have an especially hard time breaking free of the bonds of chemical dependency. It's a part of their culture and their life-style. In the best situations it may take several weeks to transform this life-style. Old friendship systems must be broken up, the drugs have to be cleaned out of their bodies, and the teenagers must renew skills and values that have lain dormant for years. Therefore, the program must be an intensive environment with no contact with old friends.

Most programs that are intensive, structured, and use a reverse positive peer pressure will be able to bring about a change in most kids for the time that they are in an all-day program. The trick comes in maintaining that change over a long period of time. In general, an effective program should include two to three months of an intensive, closed system. That could be in a hospital, a residential center, or a day treatment center that uses host homes. There should be a rigorous commitment to maintaining a drug-free atmosphere—which can be very difficult to do. Anytime you bring together a number of druggie kids, you run the danger of becoming a drug distribution center. Only through a rigorous peer confrontation system, a strong staff commitment to being drug free, and random urine screens can a treatment center protect itself from drug infiltration.

Another item to watch for with a drug-free treatment center is to what degree medications are used to maintain the kids. Very few teenage alcoholics or addicts need to be detoxified with medications. If a treatment program is using medications to "bring down" more than one or two percent of the teenagers in treatment, they may be overusing medications. Also, a lot of use of psychotropic or psychiatric medications to maintain the kids while they are in the program may indicate that the staff does not have a strong feeling about the disease concept of chemical dependency. Occasionally a teenager suffering from serious depression may need to be on antidepressants to correct that chemical imbalance. The same thing may be true of a teenager showing psychotic symptoms. I believe, however, that until young people have been drug free for several weeks, no one can have an accurate reading of where they are psychologically. Therefore, my preference is for programs that use medications very sparingly.

Gradual Reentry and Heavy Aftercare

To be able to maintain improvements over time, a program must slowly reduce the amount of time the teen spends in the program and increase the time out in the real world. There should not be an abrupt shift from being in the treatment program to "being out." The gradual reduction in interaction with the program helps the children's reentry into the real world. Going back to live with their parents, going back to public school part-time, and being able to regulate their evening and weekend activities are the kids' first tasks, and these will be where the true test of the program comes.

By the time you get to this point, you will have already invested a great deal of time and money in the program. So it is important to check into the aftercare component before you go in. Most treatment centers make most of their money in the first few weeks of the intensive program. It is not unusual for them to have trimmed back on the aftercare part to save money. A treatment center with a strong aftercare program shows a commitment to continuing quality care.

Cost of the Program

Programs vary widely in cost, and those that are more expensive are not necessarily better. A hospital program generally costs between ten and twenty thousand dollars for five or six weeks of intensive treatment and usually has a once-a-week aftercare group. It is the most expensive route to go, but it often is covered by medical insurance companies, so you may have less out-of-pocket payment. Because hospitals are expensive to run and short on space, however, they tend to concentrate on intensive initial treatment with little aftercare.

Residential centers are lower in cost per day, but treatment usually runs for a longer period of time. The longer time period results in increased residential costs, often up to fifteen to twenty-five thousand dollars. Fewer insurance companies will cover a residential facility. And since few families have fifteen to twenty-five thousand dollars to invest in treatment, there are fewer residential centers to choose from.

The newest trend in the field is toward day treatment facilities. These tend to cost much less than live-in facilities, generally costing between five and ten thousand dollars. Many insurance companies will cover up to half of the cost under their outpatient psychological services. The key to day treatment is whether the program has a host home component and can actually place teenagers outside of their own homes in their own area for a period of time. Those host homes are usually made up of families that are farther along in the program. Derrick and Theresa Clayson can attest to the effectiveness of a host-home program. "These people are family," says Derrick. "They took Aaron into their homes when we could not have stood another day with him. We've done the same with their kids and have truly grown to love them." As a parent, you want to look into the training and credibility of those families providing host homes. And with any treatment facility you want to check into the reputation of such a program in the community.

Always make sure that you see the cost up front. Ask if there are any hidden or ancillary charges. Many programs may have a three-hundred-dollar-a-day rate but charge for every specific service that comes along, making the daily rate more like four hundred to four hundred and fifty dollars. Make sure that you check with your insurance company. The insurance industry is in a time of tremendous change in regard to psychological and chemical dependency benefits. Each company differs. Some require preauthorization, some will cover only specific treatment programs, many will cover only inpatient costs, and many have maximum amounts on coverage. Do not rely on the treatment facility to explain your coverage. You should call your insurance representative yourself to make sure you know how much to depend on insurance for.

Watch your bill as it accumulates. Hospitals are under no obligation to inform you if the costs are running over what you may have expected. If your child were hospitalized for an appendectomy and developed complications, you wouldn't think twice about extending his stay for several days or a couple of weeks. You would just assume that it would be covered. That is not the case with chemical dependency benefits. Often the insurance company will allow only a certain number of days for treatment with no extensions.

If you have a child who shows early symptoms or who might be predisposed to chemical dependency and your insurance does not cover treatment for it, you would find it greatly to your benefit to shop around for better insurance coverage. Many insurance companies, especially those associated with industrial companies, have extremely good chemical dependency coverage. These companies have seen the benefits of rehabilitating long-term workers compared with having to train replacements. These companies have a much more proactive approach to their coverage of chemical dependency treatment. Often this approach includes an Employee Assistance Program (EAP) that will help you find appropriate treatment. Generally, you should steer away from HMOs (health maintenance organizations). To be able to exist in a competitive medical world, many of them have cut out the "fringe benefits," including chemical dependency and psychiatric coverage. A few, however, have excellent treatment centers within their own organizations.

Family Involvement

Chemical dependency is a disease that strikes the entire family. Even if its presence is unknown, it is still affecting every member of the household. People adapt quickly and adjust to any kind of circumstance, even the presence of a chemically dependent teenager. Such an adaptation perpetuates chemical dependency rather than discourages it. Hence, it is critical that the entire family be involved in treatment at some level. My preference is heavily in favor of programs that have either an intensive family experience for several days or extensive family involvement throughout the course of treatment. Many parents comment that they feel they have had to change more than their chemically dependent teenagers. (Chapter 9, on family dynamics, covers this topic in more depth.) The basic thrust of the family program should be to confront denial in the beginning, clarify family rules and expectations, and change the family environment to a supportive but tough climate to aid in the child's recovery.

A Strong Peer Component

As I mentioned earlier, it seems to be true that in most cases peers got your kid into drugs and peers have got to get your kid out. For an adolescent program to work, it must have a strong reverse peer culture orientation. Even though many parents of today grew up in the drug era of the sixties, today's teenagers feel that their parents know nothing about their world, especially when it comes to their drugs. They feel there is no way we can understand how pleasurable the escape is and how much fun it is to do drugs. And for many of us that's true. Beyond that, when a parent tries to give advice or instruction to a teenager, the kid often discounts it as coming from a biased source. Teenagers are often very defensive with their parents because they know that the parents have seen them from birth, good and bad. Therefore, they are especially vulnerable to any criticism that might come from a parent.

Peer relationships, on the other hand, are usually not so fraught with these apparent problems. I am constantly amazed at how much one teenager can get away with while confronting another. The druggie teens will often listen much more carefully to what another druggie teen has to say to them. The real trick is to make sure that the one doing the teaching is teaching the right things. That's why the philosophy of the treatment program is so important. By this time you know that you need any help you can get; however, you do want that help to be headed in the same direction that you are headed. At the same time, you are destined to have to rely on the judgment and advice of people you hardly know. The only way you can come to trust that advice is to get to know who these people are. Rely on what you have been told by people who have gone through the same program.

Some of the most successful programs I have seen have used higher level peers with those who are just coming into treatment. If those higher level peers are well trained and use an appropriate mix of tough love, they can speed a young teenage druggie through the denial process in much less time than it would take a group of adult therapists. Many times when I interview kids, I can feel they are stonewalling me, completely denying their drug problem. I will ask them if they would like to meet some of the kids in the program and ask questions of them, since they might feel more comfortable with someone their own age. It's not unusual, after fifteen minutes with two or three of the higher level teenagers in the program, for the new kids to offer three to five times as much drug information as I had been able to get in an hour or the parents had been able to get in two years.

The other time when this peer influence is most apparent is after a teen spends two or three days in the program. We always call a meeting with the family at this point to make sure that everyone is committed to the program. It is sometimes astonishing to see the change in the kid's attitude from day one to day three. This is primarily a result of peer influence. You need to have this kind of initial momentum to get up and out of this problem. Unless a program can demonstrate visible, relatively fast changes in attitude and appearance, the momentum will probably die in the middle stages of treatment. This rate of change is next to impossible to achieve in a program that uses only adult professionals in the treatment.

One of the main reasons that an adolescent therapeutic community works is that it gives each child a sense of belonging and meaning. The higher level kids are helping the lower level kids get started, with the expectation that they will take their place in a few months. I am firmly convinced that if all the higher level kids were to leave at one time from Dayspring, we would be right back at day one and would have to start building the treatment program completely from scratch again.

Another reason the peer component is essential is that these kids need to have a new friendship system. Our rule of thumb is that if you go back to your old using friends, you will use, every single time. There is no gray. This is a black-and-white issue. If you go back to your old using friends, you will use, every time. Consequently, the child in treatment must make a whole new system of friends. The ideal is for those kids to go back to the same school and support each other. During your investigation of a program, you will want to see if the treatment program has ways of reentering kids in support groups in the schools they came from. If while in treatment they don't establish some very tight friendships, they will almost invariably return to the people who were their friends before. In those cases their chance of recovery drops to below ten percent.

The step into treatment is one of the most important that you will ever make in your life. Make sure that you do some shopping around. The following list will help to ensure that you have found the best treatment possible for your chemically dependent teenager.

Treatment Checklist

Does the program treat chemical dependency as a primary disease?

Is the program intensive and carefully structured, with specific requirements for the recovering child?

Does the program maintain a strictly drug-free environment? How frequently are the participants given other kinds of medication?

Does the program allow the child to reenter the "real world" in a gradual fashion?

What are the aftercare components of the program? Will there be ongoing support?

What does the program cost? Are the costs clear? How much will insurance cover?

Is the entire family involved in the recovery process?

Does the program have a strong peer component?

Does the program have a strong connection with the schools?

Section 2

UNDERLYING ISSUES

Chapter 7

STRESS AND THE INDIVIDUAL

Getting off drugs and staying off is not just a one-time decision that, once made, sets the addict free for life. Coming clean involves a whole new way of looking at life, and one of the primary changes a person must make is in how he or she deals with stress.

Stress is a major ingredient in drug abuse among teenagers today. We saw in chapter 2 that our society has become increasingly complex and that knowledge has exploded while personal relationships have largely disappeared. A young person trying to find a niche in today's world feels a tremendous sense of overload.

We have to teach our children how to cope with the world in which they live. This knowledge can be preventive as well as curative: a kid who has learned healthy ways of dealing with stress is less likely to turn to drugs in the first place. And the kid who already has a drug problem can be taught that there is another way—a better, more productive way—to get through life.

How can we convey this essential life skill? I like to use an analogy—a modern-day parable, if you will—about the complexities of our world and how we deal with them. Our kids have all spent plenty of time at the arcade playing Space Invaders. We can draw many parallels between the popular video game and the game of day-to-day living.

The Rules of the Game

The game Space Invaders is made up of several columns of little creatures that march down from the sky, and the purpose of the game is to shoot them before they shoot you. We could liken these columns to the different areas of stress in our lives. For adults, the first column might be job-related stresses; the second, handling finances; the third, managing a home; the fourth, family; and the fifth, friends or social life. For the adolescent the columns in figure 1 might be labeled family, school, friends, and so on.

Five rules apply in this game that I think are critical in understanding the stress that adults and adolescents are under.

Rules

1. No win—they never stop coming
2. The more you improve, the harder the game gets.
3. We have limited energy and resources.
4. No escape.
5. The challenge: become proactive instead of reactive.

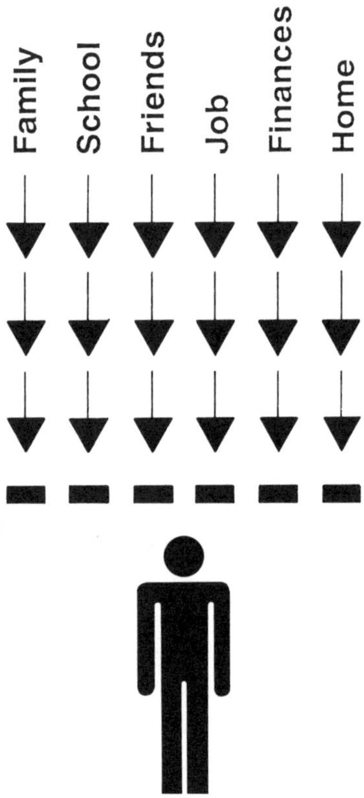

Figure 1. Space Invaders

Rule One: No Win—They Never Stop Coming

In the game Space Invaders, no matter how many times you shoot down the little creatures that are coming at you, more will always follow. If you shoot down the first wave of space invaders, there will always be a second wave.

The application to real life is easily seen. Think about the number of times you have sat down to pay bills. Yet, no matter how many times you pay those bills, in a couple of weeks there will always be more bills to pay. For a teenager, no matter how many assignments the kid gets done, there will always be more to do. Dishes will continue to be dirtied, grass will continue to grow and need mowing—until the winter, when snow will pile up to be shoveled instead. Depressing, isn't it? For many, the fact that the space invaders never stop makes life seem like a no-win situation. We have the conception that success in life, or in anything, means finally getting the space invaders to stop. As we get used to the game, we realize that what actually happens is that we have short periods of rest and then the space invaders are there for us to take on again.

We need to understand, however, that stress is an extremely important ingredient in our personal growth. Take a look at our lives from the very first second that we entered the world. We squeezed down a very long, dark tube, popped out into bright sunlight, and somebody in a white coat picked us up by one of our legs and gave us a quick pop on the bottom—and somewhere deep inside we knew that the quarter had just gone into the machine and our game had begun. We found ourselves going through all sorts of stress: getting hungry, crying, and seeing that the world was going to have a lot of requirements for us; yet at the same time inside of us was this gnawing need, pulling us toward new experiences that would create stress and at the same time provide us with fulfillment.

When I was working for the welfare department in protective services, I came across many babies who had been taken out of their homes because they had been neglected or abused. In many of those cases, the only problem that existed was that Mom never did anything to create stress in the baby's life. She just left the baby in the bed, feeding it and changing it occasionally, but in general she was feeling so overwhelmed with life that she couldn't do anything to really give that baby any affection. A baby in this situation will develop a syndrome called "failure to thrive." This syndrome is brought about when parents leave a baby totally to itself without giving it any touching or loving, without having any requirements for it. Babies with failure-to-thrive syndrome can easily die if someone does not take them and change their life-style. When such a child is put into a new home, the new parents are excited, and they jostle the baby about and play with it and wake it up to talk to numbers of people—things that we might consider to be very stressful. Yet under these conditions there is typically a remarkable turnaround in that baby's desire to live.

We can draw the conclusion that all of us need a certain amount of stress, or challenge, to be able to grow. The real key, as we will see later, is how we define that experience, whether we can see it as a challenge or whether it becomes a burden that constantly overloads us.

Rule Two: The More We Improve, the Harder the Game Gets

When we become proficient enough at Space Invaders to wipe out the whole first wave of creatures, what happens to them? Does the game get easier, or does it get harder? As you know if you are a video buff, when you get better, the game gets more challenging. The space invaders start coming faster, and in many of the games the board increases in complexity and adds new elements to the game. Think about that as it applies to your life.

Do you remember back in high school when you thought that your life was about as complex as it could possibly get? There were the life-shaking issues of boyfriends, girlfriends, algebra, the prom. And yet as you got older and began to add things like a job, a house, a spouse, and children, you realized that life got more complex each time you added a new column of space invaders. Most of us have a bad habit of underestimating how much more complicated our lives will become with each new column of stress.

For example, most of us when we got married had very little idea of what would be required in that relationship. We had gotten overloaded and sick of the level of the game that we were currently playing and really needed something else to fulfill our lives. Many of us move into jobs and children and new houses with the same underestimation of how much time and energy we will need to truly be able to conquer that particular space invader. Few of us, however, would go back to the level of simplicity that we had before.

It can be depressing to realize that life is always getting more complex every time we make another advancement. But would we continue to play the game if it didn't? What would happen if the game of Space Invaders always stayed at the first level, if every wave came at the same speed, and if each one had the same level of complexity? Soon we would become bored. We need those added challenges.

There are many people in my neighborhood who look longingly toward the mountains all autumn, hoping for the first snowfall. Then, after the white stuff has begun to accumulate on those mountain peaks, they get all bundled up like walking sleeping bags and head for the mountains. They go up into the cold, the wind, and the snow and ride on little metal chairs high above the ground that take them to the top of steep, snow-covered cliffs. Then, with flat pieces of slick wood and fiberglass strapped to their feet, they slide down at speeds that are a threat to their very lives. Every day you will see people along the side with broken bones and sprains, being carried off in small toboggans to hospitals where they will spend the rest of the winter in casts and Ace bandages. And they pay twenty-five dollars a day for the privilege of adding this massive space invader—skiing—to their lives. Are you beginning to see that the key to conquering the game has something to do with how we define our space invaders?

Rule Three: We Live with Limited Energy and Resources

One of the most frustrating things about the game of life is that there are unlimited space invaders, but we have to function with limited energy and limited resources. As we play, our energy and ability to concentrate gradually begin to fade. Our efficiency deteriorates, and soon we find the space invaders running all over us, and our score is so embarrassing we don't want anyone else to see how we finished up. At some point we overload and don't want to have anything else to do with the game.

We also run out of quarters pretty easily. Few of us have the resources that allow us to spend our money on whatever we want. We often find ourselves at the end of a pay period running out of those resources and feeling that tremendous sense of overload. As we look at this third rule, one of the factors of drug abuse will begin to make more sense to us.

Let's look at our daily energy pattern. At some point in the morning, most of us who keep regular hours will experience our peak energy level. During this peak we will find ourselves evaluating the day, looking at the space invaders, and deciding what we need to get done. As the day progresses, however, we experience a predictable drop in energy, and as we reach ten or eleven o'clock at night, we begin to feel the overload of the space invaders. Our energy has dropped to a nonfunctioning level, and yet the space invaders are still there to be taken care of. We begin not to care anymore; we just can't deal with one more space invader. Most of us start looking for flat mats in dark rooms where we go and cover ourselves with pieces of cloth and soon descend into a blissful, depressed condition in which we block out the entire world. But if we're painfully aware of big space invaders that are approaching, we'll have a hard time making that descent. Eventually, though, the overload rule wins out, and we slip into this depressed coma, unable to deal with any space invaders until we have recharged our batteries. The next day we arise from this recharging posture to face the space invaders again.

The catch is that most of us do not go through a nice, predictable decline from eight o'clock in the morning to ten o'clock at night. Instead, we experience a more up-and-down energy pattern. At various periods throughout the day we feel our energy level dropping and that overloaded feeling pressing in. Have you found yourself in that condition around two or three o'clock in the afternoon? Depending on how we handle such a slump, we may find ourselves recharging back up the rest of the afternoon, or slipping down into one of those depressed comas, or reaching out to find something that will bolster us up and keep us going through the day. That is where drug abuse becomes a real factor and a cause for concern in our society.

Let's take one of the times of highest risk during the day: the hour from five until six o'clock when people are getting home from work. The local bars advertise this as "happy hour"; as a marriage and family therapist I would label it the "arsenic hour." Mom and Dad come home from work; they're tired; they're shifting from one set of stresses to another. Most people have a set routine for shifting gears from the work space invaders to the home ones. Johnny, coming home from school, will be in the same situation. He's trying to forget about his homework, to shift from being in school to having a good time and making his life more fulfilling during those evening hours. It is often at this risky time, when we feel as if we are in a downward spiral and need to shift our focus and forget the space invaders of our work world, that we find ourselves engaging in unhealthy escapes.

What do you do when you come home from work and are shifting gears to begin the evening hours? For many Americans, that hour after work means coming in and putting on their most comfortable slippers, sitting down to read the paper, and turning on the television to watch the evening news. Many of us raid the refrigerator, putting anything into our mouths that will fit. Others drop off to sleep during that time or make the transition by listening to music. Many people, however, will reach for a beer, a glass of wine, or a quick cocktail. The ingestion of alcohol at this time produces a predictable effect that they think helps them shift gears. Johnny will more likely slip down into the basement and smoke a joint.

Each one of these escape activities, including the alcohol and drug use, sets off a similar pattern. Whenever a person is napping, eating, listening to music, reading, or ingesting alcohol or drugs, there will be a quick, predictable, sensory "high" followed by a rapid drop-off in consciousness. Sleep is the prototype of the kind of escape we are talking about. Think about a Sunday afternoon nap: you slip your toes between those sheets and feel that euphoric burst of sensory relief in which your entire body just seems to yell "ahhh." That pleasurable sensory high is usually followed by a rapid drop-off in consciousness.

Let's apply this sequence to eating food for emotional reasons. Jane comes into the kitchen feeling anxious; she opens up the refrigerator and begins to empty it into her mouth. It is amazing how good everything tastes when a person is hungry and anxious. She has that sensory high feeling. Then, after eating that entire pizza left over from last night, how does she feel in about fifteen minutes? She feels full, her torso feels warm, she feels sluggish, and pretty soon she's sitting in front of the television dozing off to sleep. Jane has just engaged in a predictable escape process and has altered her consciousness through the ingestion of food.

The same process happens with the ingestion of alcohol or drugs. There will be a predictable, easy, sensory high followed by an equally predictable, rapid drop-off in consciousness. Just about every drug will provide us with that kind of an experience. We can get hooked on the high as well as on the drop-off.

To summarize, then, rule three is that we have limited energy and resources and at least once a day will drop off to the point of total unconsciousness where we spend about one-third of our existence. The problem is that often our energy level drops off sometime during the middle of the day. When that happens and we feel overloaded, we often reach for some kind of sensory escape. That gets us to rule number four.

Rule Four: No Escape

In the game Space Invaders, when the heat begins to build and we want to escape, we slide over behind one of the little shields and sit there for a period of time. While we're hiding there, however, do the space invaders go away? No. The problem is that while we are hiding from the space invaders, they are working away on our shields and eventually erode their way through. Think about this in relation to your life. If you don't make your car payment, the bank is not going to just let it slide by. While you are worrying over where you are going to find the money to make the car payment, those nasty little late notices and late charges are piling up on your desk. The intrusion of one of those little space invaders into your life can make you feel overloaded and depressed, which just makes you want to hide more.

As the space invaders pile up deeper and deeper on our shields, the pressure eventually reaches the point where they break through, and we have that instant revelation that we are in deep trouble. Then we wish beyond hope that we had taken care of this thing a long time ago. Adolescents go through this process daily. We all learned in our teens how to put off assignments until the final week when everything was due. Then we would cram for the tests and stay up all night to get the papers done.

When the space invaders finally do break through our shields, we end up flailing across the board in panic mode, trying to get them before they get us. We seldom work efficiently in this mode and will never find ourselves reaching that expert level where we are in control of the game instead of having it control us. The shields don't solve anything—they just postpone the problems until they get too big to ignore.

Drugs serve as a shield for teenagers to hide behind so that they don't have to come out and face the stress of playing the game and fighting the space invaders. I appeared recently on a television talk show where teenagers were asked what some of their major problems were and why they used drugs. Several of them said that they thought their parents put too many demands on them. I thought many of them were missing the fact that the game itself puts a great many demands on a person. Most of them were accustomed to living in nice homes, having cars, and enjoying a tremendous amount of freedom, all provided by their parents' fighting a lot of space invaders to get those things. Our kids would love to find ways to escape from the responsibilities of life. Everything they see in the movies, on television, and in music suggests that adults are ripping off their lives by putting undue expectations on them. Teenagers would give everything to receive all the rewards of middle-class life without having to do any work to get them. It is critical for adolescents to understand the no-escape rule and also to realize that you and I have to play the game right along with them.

The major battle that we have as parents is to try to teach our kids the difference between long-term rewards, or deferred gratification, and instant gratification. Our kids want *what* they want *when* they want it. They're experts at knowing how to plan and carry off the short-range escapes in their lives. They have little conception of the long-term rewards that can come through getting excited about playing the game.

One of the biggest problems with using drugs as an escape is that all drugs operate on a principle called tolerance. Tolerance can best be described in relation to the game as the shields getting thinner and thinner the more a kid uses the same drug. The drug, as a shield, or an escape, becomes less effective with continued use.

Here's another example: Have you ever found yourself craving a particular kind of ice cream? You mentally inventory where the local ice cream places are, which ones feature the flavor you are instinctively drawn to, and soon you are driving to one particular ice cream parlor. The first lick of that pralines and cream or double chocolate chip provides you with the maximum sensory experience.

Now let's say that you enjoyed that cone so much that you went back the next day and had another one—same flavor. Was it as good as it seemed yesterday? Would it continue to be as good if you went back every day of the month and had the same flavor of ice cream? That is the principle of tolerance at work: as you continue to use the same substance over and over again, your body and your mind begin to become tolerant to the escape and the pleasurable effect that you had upon first use.

Complicating things even further is that all drugs, and escapes, have what is called a toxic level. The toxic level can be defined as the point at which your body and mind are unable to deal with a particular substance. With drugs this is described as an overdose. To go back to the ice cream example, suppose that in your efforts to recapture the sensory high you enjoyed with your very first ice cream cone, you purchased and consumed an entire gallon of that flavor of ice cream. You would experience a saturation effect, and you probably wouldn't be able to stomach one more spoonful of that stuff for quite a while. If you pushed your system to eat more, you might regret it. You have reached your toxic level.

As we have shown, when tolerance builds, the need for more of the substance grows. Over time the tolerance effect will cause the amount of drugs a person takes to climb closer and closer to the toxic level. Eventually those two levels will meet and precipitate a tremendous crisis in the user's life. Tolerance is the principle that makes it impossible for anyone to abuse a substance, especially drugs, for any period of time without experiencing a major crisis.

Game—or formula for suicide? Why would anybody of sound mind play this Space Invaders game, knowing that the rules were that you would never win because there were always more space invaders; that the better you got, the harder the game would get; that you have only limited energy and resources and will always overload to the point of apathy and depression; that no matter how much you would like to escape from the space invaders, you can only get away for short periods of time, and ultimately there is no escape?

The first four rules of this game are very depressing. In fact, for the adolescent who is trying to become an adult and is just learning the rules, these four can serve as a formula for suicide. The teenager (or the adult) develops a sense of hopelessness, a feeling that there is no light at the end of the tunnel, and finally, sitting down at the side of the road, decides that there is really no reason to keep on moving. And that is the function that drug abuse has served for so many teenagers today.

So why do we continue to play the game? It's true that the rates of adolescent suicide are rising rapidly, but still the great majority of our teens choose to remain here and play the game in one fashion or another. What is the purpose of the game? What is it in human nature that continues to allure many of us to be excited about life, excited about jobs, excited about school? That brings us to rule number five.

Rule Five: The Challenge

The only thing that makes this game worth playing, considering the first four rules, is the challenge of it all, the idea of taking what we have been given and making more of it. Each of us is built with this internal, inherited desire to make the most of ourselves, to grow, to become independent, to become successful, to gain the respect and the love of those around us. The problem comes with the tremendous amount of work it takes to get there. Take physical fitness as a good example. If you want to make a muscle stronger, you must exercise and strain that muscle. If the muscle is allowed to stay relaxed, with no stress and no strain over a long period of time, it will eventually atrophy and die. Human beings are the same way. If we don't continue to exercise ourselves toward some kind of a goal, we too will atrophy and die. This principle of challenge is at the heart of human motivation.

Let's look at the game of Space Invaders again. What motivates us to continue the game, to keep playing it time and time again, to try to improve ourselves? It could be the idea of just shooting down more and more space invaders, maybe of eventually shooting down one of those little flying saucers that goes across the top. It could be the idea of finally making it into that third or fourth wave that we have never been to before. I think, however, that one of the things that makes video games especially addicting to us is that they give us a very specific score as we play. As simple as it may seem, the score is essential to our continuing to be motivated to play the game. It allows us to see exactly where we are, whether we are improving, and how we rank against other people who are playing the game.

Reactive Life-style

- Is aware of only the first four rules
- Always feels overloaded
- Scrambles to play the game
- Unable to look ahead and plan
- Starts tasks with a sense of dread

Proactive Life-style

- Focuses on rule five: Life is a challenge
- Develops goals, strategies, and evaluates progress along the road
- Predicts and plans ahead—anticipates
- Focuses on the score and not the endless space invaders

Figure 2. The choice between a proactive or a reactive life-style

To enjoy the challenge of life's game, we need to learn to keep score. Figure 2 depicts the score in each major area of a person's life as a bar graph. How are you doing? For most of us, it's pretty easy to determine our financial score. And in our homes we can redecorate the basement, add on another room, or build new shelves in the garage, all of which lead to some sense of accomplishment. With our jobs, however, it's becoming increasingly more complicated to find some sense of reward and accomplishment. Many times the only reward I can see is that one set of papers has moved from the left side of my desk to the right side. With the advent of computers, this accomplishment has become even less visible: perhaps a whole day's work is represented by a bunch of magnetic digits on a disk.

Contrast that with your great-grandparents and their plowed fields. At the end of the day Grandpa could sit down and look back at that field and see the fruit of his labor stretching across a vast expanse. Most families had a fairly large plot of ground that made up their homestead. Every piece of work could be seen as a betterment of their own personal space.

Of course, few of us would really like to go back to that age. Most of us like our dishwashers and washing machines and motor vehicles. But with our rich, specialized, complex society, we must work harder at being able to visualize the rewards and the score in order to keep up our motivation to play the game.

Perhaps an even more perplexing area for us in regard to score and motivation comes in our relationships. I can see a promotion or a salary increase much more clearly than I can see the progress I might have made toward being a better husband. In areas with less tangible rewards, we have to work even harder to make sure that we are progressing and feeling challenged by the experience. And yet, it's worth the effort. As a marriage counselor, I have seen over and over again that all the success in the business world will not make up for failure in relationships with spouses and children. As we get older, those relationships become more and more important in our value systems. But we have to plan our motivations more carefully and make our goals much more specific. This is the change in attitude that we spoke of at the beginning of this chapter, the life skill of wanting to act instead of being acted upon. Another phrase we might use to describe these two contrasting life-styles is reactive versus proactive.

The Reactive Life-style

A person with a reactive life-style is typically aware only of the first four rules of life's game. Such a person begins each day with a sense of being overloaded, a sense of dread, and often a sense of anger at the unfairness of the rules of the game. Reactive people will ignore the possibility that they could choose to feel stimulated by the challenge instead of overwhelmed by it. They will tend to blame others for the way that their own lives are progressing. They feel as if everybody else is shoving the space invaders down their throat, that they have no responsibility for their problems. Those people then express hopelessness, confusion, and bitterness even at God for making life such a mess.

All of us become reactive sometimes. Anytime we become reactive, however, we invariably do things that will cause us to fail. Reactivity thus becomes a self-perpetuating phenomenon. We get angry because of the unlimited space invaders and our lack of energy to be able to deal with them, so we reactively use up all our energy in anger and bitterness and depression, which puts us even farther behind the space invaders. Depression, particularly, is a good example. I feel overloaded because I have too much to do. Consequently, I find some escape to make me feel better and to take my mind off all the space invaders. After having engaged in that escape, I feel guilty for not having been responsible in facing the space invaders, and I also find myself even further behind. This makes me feel more depressed, so I seek more escapes, feel more guilty, become more depressed, and so on. The only way I can break that downward spiral is to make a conscious decision to change my life-style.

The Proactive Life-style

One of the most important decisions you or your child will ever make is to see life as a challenge rather than as something to be dreaded. We must become excited about the concept of taking what we've got and scoring higher. A proactive life-style is exemplified by the person who looks forward to the next day. The proactive person sets goals, figures out a direction or way to achieve them, estimates the energy and resources it will take to get to each goal, and then has enough faith to be able to endure over a period of time to attain the goal.

It can be difficult for someone who has lived a life of reactive behavior to suddenly make a change and become proactive; however, I emphasize again that becoming proactive is a conscious choice. At some point you must decide that being proactive is the kind of life-style you want, that you are sick and tired of being sick and tired, and that being excited and having some sense of faith about your life takes no more energy than being reactive and depressed. Perhaps the most critical decision you will ever make is to change your focus from believing that the first four rules are the only things that exist in life to believing in the challenge and the excitement that lie before you.

There are several steps you can take to develop a proactive life-style. Each one of those steps is critical to the process of turning things around. The first step involves shifting your focus toward the score and away from the endless waves. You must appreciate what you already have and build on it. I think one of the greatest sins of our day is that we don't appreciate what we have until we lose it. If our kids had a greater sense of awe at how good we have it in this life, even with all its complexity, far fewer of them would be depressed and chemically dependent. That's also true of us adults. When we start to appreciate what we have, then we have a foundation to build on. If all we can do is focus on the space invaders that we still haven't dealt with and keep reminding ourselves of how far behind we are and how little energy we have, we will never have any kind of solid foundation.

The second step is giving yourself permission to dream and to build goals. God gave us an inherent ability to reach beyond our current state. Often we discourage children from dreaming by being critical and labeling them as selfish. It's true that if the developmental process stops here and doesn't go on to action, the child who dreams can become selfish and lazy. But I think that learning how to dream is a critical element in becoming proactive. If you don't have something to reach for, it's hard to make yourself reach at all. We need to reestablish this ability.

The third step to proactivity involves taking your dreams and making them measurable and attainable—in other words, developing a strategy for attaining those dreams. What are our interim goals, or interim space invaders, that we'll have to deal with to get there? Kids who are considered experts at the game of Space Invaders all have a strategy about how to fight their way through the waves of space invaders to get to the third, fourth, and fifth levels. As I look at my successful friends, I notice that all of them have the ability to dream, but they also have the ability to create strategies for getting to a particular goal.

The fourth step in developing a proactive life-style is to find some way to measure your progress. Few really worthwhile goals can be achieved in a short time. Most of the things that build a person's self-image take a long time to accomplish. We must have some mechanism in place by which we can see ourselves working through the different stages toward attaining our goals. We need mile markers along the way so that we can stop occasionally and realize that we are indeed making progress.

The fifth and final step is that you must have an internal belief in something greater than yourself if you are to maintain enough internal energy and faith to keep moving down this long road. In these days of tremendous complexity, it is impossible for us to take into account all of our stress-inducing variables at one time. While we are working on one column of space invaders, we need some sense of confidence that we don't have to worry about all the others at the same time. That is where a belief in God is so critical to most young people's recovery from chemical dependency. Such a belief allows them the freedom to concentrate on one area of their lives at a time, to be able to conquer that one before moving on to the next. Almost all successful people have developed that kind of focusing faith; people who have become disabled and helpless often worry about all the columns of space invaders at the same time. That is like trying to play the game without any shields and without any respite—trying to fight all the stressors all the time. That is next to impossible. The space invaders have to be dealt with one at a time, and although we need to have an overall strategy about how we will eventually take care of the entire wave, we need to recognize that we won't do it in one fell swoop.

People who follow these five steps and who are continually working to improve their abilities in each one are living a proactive life-style. It is my firm conviction that people who consciously commit themselves to a proactive life-style and are doing everything they can to move away from a reactive life-style will find themselves moving up to a level of happiness and productivity that they never dreamed they could accomplish. We must teach our children these principles; otherwise, they will be constantly aware of the first four rules of the game, they will feel overwhelmed, helpless, and bitter, and eventually they will turn to escapes that will ensure their failure.

Chapter 8

SPIRITUALITY

We have identified overload from stress as one of the main components in teenage drug use; however, there is another factor that most likely supersedes all other causes. That factor is the lack of spirituality among our youth. Spirituality can have many different meanings, depending on culture, background, and experience. In this context, I will use spirituality in a rather generic sense, as defining your meaning in life, having a sense of a "higher power," or God, whom you can rely on, and having a personal faith that allows you to endure through the stresses in hopes that there will be a reward for the effort in the long run.

Meaning in Life

"What good is a teenager, anyway?" The question may sound rude, but it is an important one. It used to be that children went through ceremonies that signified the end of childhood and the beginning of adulthood. Survival in those older cultures was a priority in day-to-day existence: the more children who became functioning adults, the better the group's chances of survival. Today, however, we have evolved a life of luxury in which survival is seldom a major issue. We truly do not need our youths to help us survive. We have transformed their position in the family. Whereas they used to be an essential component, critical to the survival of the family, now the family has to make up jobs for them. Our teenagers know that we rely on them for very little, and since they have few real responsibilities, they have taken these adolescent years and turned them into the last time in their lives when they can party and still be supported by their parents. We've given them so much as parents that they feel they have nothing to contribute to us and indeed, in most cases, that has become true.

The latter end of the twentieth century is going to present increasing challenges for parents to depend on their children in ways that will make the kids feel like an integral part of the family. As long as they feel like appendages, they will feel they have nothing to lose by getting involved in such destructive practices as alcohol and drug abuse.

This principle is as true in our school system and our churches as it is in our families. Most churches are losing their young people in great numbers. The dropout rate in schools is becoming greater and greater across the country. One of the reasons is that teenagers feel no ownership in the systems they belong to. We must become innovative in the ways that we use teenagers in these systems. We must find ways for young people to lead and take responsibility for more areas at church, at school, and in the family.

The only way teenagers can feel more power and responsibility in the social organizations to which they belong is if the adult leaders are willing to relinquish some of their power. The idea of teenagers taking more responsibility is very appealing to us, until we realize that it will cost us some of our own personal power. In church, for instance, many of us adults find our meaning in life by being "youth leaders." The youth need to become their own leaders, under the wise but sometimes distant supervision of us adults.

At Dayspring we have a strong reverse peer culture. A number of the graduates of the program come back to serve as staff. Throughout the different phases of treatment, the kids must show more and more leadership with the kids who are new in the program. The reason they are willing to spend the time helping someone else out is that they feel a tremendous ownership in what they are doing. For them to have that ownership, my staff and I must give up some of our power and control. The supervision must be careful and loving and strategic, but it must give them enough freedom to feel ownership. That is a critical factor in successful parenting, in running a successful church program, and in running a successful school. We must give up some of our power and control, becoming better supervisors and facilitators and allowing the kids to take ownership and responsibility.

Building a Personal Faith

Meaning in life comes from having an effect on the world that surrounds you. To be able to do that successfully, you must struggle your way through the stress and be patient enough to wait for the results. If you have done any gardening, you know that you must do the labor to cultivate, plant, fertilize, and water your crops. But the results will never be instantaneous. You have to have the faith to wait out the natural process that will lead your garden to bear fruit.

That faith must be a positive, hopeful attitude toward life. It is feeling a sense of challenge instead of a sense of dread, feeling a desire to master your universe and become better rather than just to kick back and escape all the time. Our children seem to be easily discouraged by the amount of work that is required to bring about anything worthwhile. They are exposed all day long to media messages suggesting that the most worthwhile things in life are being able to escape and get away from it all. Society has come up with a sophisticated set of escapes that make our children feel good and pleasurable instantly and constantly. When it comes to the really big tasks, like moving out into the world, getting married, or finding a higher meaning in life, they usually become discouraged and sit down and quit.

One factor that complicates young people's search for personal faith today is that those instantaneous escapes are becoming available to them at earlier and earlier ages. The average age of first drug use is between twelve and twelve and one-half years old. Most kids begin experimenting with drugs in the seventh or eighth grade. But most of us are not expecting them to make a solid decision about their own personal faith until they are sixteen to eighteen years old. In this society, by the time a child has reached that age, a tremendous amount of water has already gone under the bridge. We parents need to start expecting our children to come up with their own personal faith by the time they are twelve or thirteen years old. Our church classes need to be geared toward helping young people make that kind of decision at that early an age. This is the only advantage I can think of in having the drug situation as problematic as it is today: it is forcing our children at very early ages to grow up and decide how they're going to motivate their lives. It may bring about a revolution in our schools and churches if we see young people beginning to take ownership in their own values and their own faith.

Believing in a Higher Power

One of the things that caught me off guard when I came into the field of drug rehabilitation was the emphasis on spirituality. I had come from a background in mental health where most clinics were funded by federal dollars and talking about spirituality was taboo. But most private programs employ the philosophy of Alcoholics Anonymous, which has a very strong spiritual base. In fact, one of the first steps in treatment is to identify your need for a higher power and then to "give your life and your will over to God as you understand him." We allow our kids in treatment to pick out whatever higher power they truly feel that they can rely on. Many are angry at God, angry at their churches, and angry at their parents, and they do not want to voice any concept of God as they have grown up understanding him. Therefore, many of them pick the group or a sponsor or some cause as their higher power to begin with. Invariably, however, most kids who are successful in treatment begin to identify their higher power as the God they grew up with. They begin to pray and to show signs of hope that somebody up there is helping them to organize the higher issues that they don't understand right now. This faith in their higher power allows them to unload a tremendous burden that they have been carrying around with them for a long time. It allows them to work on one problem at a time, so that they can keep their concentration focused and finish each small task that they set out to do. They rely on God to help with the overall strategy. For most of them, this approach works very effectively.

Most kids who get involved with drugs will throw off the church that they grew up with. It's very important for parents to realize that it may take a good deal of time for the kids to work back through the rebelliousness and the resentment that they feel toward their church. Churches complicate things by not knowing how to deal with druggie kids. Many people behave inappropriately, showing tremendous anger or fear if this kid tries to be a part of youth activities.

A step toward spirituality and a step toward God are definitely a move back in the right direction. It's important for parents to have just as much faith and patience as they are asking their children to have. In other words, let them move one step at a time back toward the value system that you would prefer for them to have. It may take them years to sort out their ambivalence and to make a decision on their own about just how far back into religion they will go. Some paradoxes are involved at this stage. An old AA saying is one of them: "Let go and let God." You might have to let go of your emotions about getting Janey back to church in order for her to be able to feel the freedom to choose it for herself. Many times in treatment we have seen parents let go of the strong desire to pull the child back into their church, only to see that child initiate interest on his or her own a few weeks later. In chapter 5 we discussed the process of strategic withdrawal, in which the parents pull back from the child in hopes that their absence will motivate that child to step back toward the family. Almost all churches have recourse to some sort of withdrawal, generally called disfellowshipment or excommunication. Ideally this process is done in love and great patience, with the hope that the member will feel the loss of the relationships and step back toward conformity to the church's rules. We as parents will have to practice the same principles if we are to give our children the freedom to make their own spiritual choices and to feel a real sense of ownership of their spirituality, or a personal testimony.

The Problem of Free Agency

A very difficult spiritual principle to deal with is the concept of free agency. God allows us freedom of choice. Without it we would be only puppets, with no ability to choose our own destiny. With it, we are able to feel that ownership discussed earlier, that we have made our own choices and will take our own consequences. Free agency is the key concept in raising children. It used to be that we could wait until they were seventeen or eighteen before we really had to wrestle with the difficulties of free agency, letting our children make their own choices and deal with the consequences themselves. That is not the case today. Strategic withdrawal is much more difficult when the child involved is only twelve, but the parents must recognize that they cannot control the choices that their children make. As parents, we can only influence. Many times our influencing will bring about results opposite from those we desire, but we must do everything we can to make sure our children understand the consequences of their decisions. Our job is to make their choices clear. If we have fulfilled our responsibility to do everything we can to teach them the results of the different directions they might go, it's time to let go and have them make their own choices. This letting go may mean that we can no longer have the child living with us. It may mean that the kid will return to drugs. It may even mean that the child will die. Our job is to influence for as long as we can, but then the time will come when we must truly let go and let God.

Many parents feel guilty because their children don't turn out the way they thought they would or should. God never gives us any guarantees. If we were to have guarantees, there would be no free agency. In scripture you will find that many godly parents lost their children through the children's exercising their free agency. God does give us some direction about how to raise the odds that our kids will turn out better. But he allows for their free agency, and so must we. We must recognize that his batting average with us is not too good. If a critic were to evaluate God's parenting ability by how well we were doing as his children down here, he could conclude that God is not the best parent, because most of us are not doing what God wants us to do. I think God has made it clear that he doesn't expect everyone to make it because he has said, "Strait is the gate, and narrow is the way, which leadeth unto life, and few there be that find it." (Matthew 7:14.) But he has put us here to see which of us will use our free agency to choose to follow his counsel and make the most of our lives while we are here. There are no guarantees in parenting, only honest principles that will increase the chances that our children will make the right choices.

Honesty and Trusting in Truth

The first rule of drug treatment is rigorous honesty. When children with drug problems begin to go through rehabilitation, the first goal is to get them to trust in telling the truth. That is very difficult for drug users, because they have relied for so long on deception and lying. They have often suffered no immediate consequences for lying their way through a situation, so many of them feel that there is no advantage in telling the truth. Again, it is only from a spiritual base of trusting something greater than yourself that you can see the long-term benefit of being rigorously honest. Most parents believe that children will grow up with a feeling that honesty is better than deception. That's just not the case. For kids who are interested only in immediate results and who feel they have nothing to lose, deception and lying can be a functional tool. It is up to us to show them that if they value anything in their future, they must rigorously uphold the truth.

Kids often believe that the definition of truth is "whatever works." This isn't a bad definition as long as we're looking at things with a long-term perspective. Indeed, as we grow older and wiser, we see that truths are principles, teachings, and practices that allow us to achieve our hearts' deepest dreams. Many of us believe that truth comes from

God and can be found in scripture. For our children, however, scriptures just seem like empty words that have not helped them deal with peer pressure or achieve success in their lives. Jesus worked very hard in his teaching to take true principles and put them into everyday applications. He did that by teaching in parables. Parents must take the God-given truths they have learned and translate them into modern-day applications that will be relevant to their children. The Space Invaders story in chapter 7 is a form of a parable. It takes a modern-day picture that children can relate to and applies to it true principles, or rules, that children are going to face in growing up. Our children don't believe in truth because they don't understand truth. It is our task to bring it down to their level so they can understand and practice true principles. When they start to see the benefit of following truths, they will begin to practice them on their own.

Love, the Bull's-eye to Shoot For

The spiritual principle that transcends all others is that we are here on this earth to learn how to love one another better. Scripture tells us to love our neighbors as ourselves. As humans, we have the instinct to develop close companionship with each other. All of us need other people. That's why this principle is so important. Getting along with each other and learning how to love one another are not just good ideas—they are the bull's-eye of the target that we are shooting for. Motivation and success are essential to our lives. Learning to be honest and to find the truth in the principles that we live is also important. But none of those things matter if they are not experienced in a context of loving and caring about other people and about God.

The Apostle Paul summarizes this principle beautifully in 1 Corinthians 13, his great discourse on charity, or the pure love of Christ. He points out that you may be able to accomplish phenomenal feats, and you may be able to give unselfishly of everything that you have, even your own life, but if you don't do it out of love, then it's nothing. I think the real hope for recovery for a drug addict, or for preventing drug abuse from happening with young people, is measured by their capacity to love and care for the people around them.

The greatest thing about working in a treatment program is to see a child become drug free and, after weeks of intensively relating to other young people, to see him or her begin to soften and reach out to other kids in the program. It's an exhilarating experience. If there were only one simple principle that I could give you as a bull's-eye to shoot for, it would be to teach your children how to truly love. That is the greatest spiritual principle, and the greatest key to prevention of drug abuse, that exists.

Chapter 9

FAMILY DYNAMICS

"How do you handle it when you watch your kid heading down the street carrying a black garbage bag with a few clothes in it? You hope he'll come crawling home in a few days, finally appreciating what you provide. But instead you hear he's sleeping at a friend's house, and then you get your country club bill and find out he's been eating just fine." Mark Obert speaks wryly.

"After each disappointment you convince yourself that it won't happen again—that you've finally been successful as a parent and can let down. You can survive on that denial for a long time," says Christine Obert.

In the summer of 1983, Mark Obert took his sons, John and Roger, along with their grandfather to San Carlos Bay, Mexico, for the fishing trip of a lifetime. Their condominium was on the beach only yards from the shore; a fishing boat sat waiting in the harbor. "I was in heaven," Mark says. "I remember thinking then that I couldn't be happier. The boys were eleven and twelve. A perfect time, I thought, to create the same kind of bond with my sons that I shared with my father."

In the summer of 1986, Mark Obert was on the telephone with the owner of a local skateboard shop. "It's past midnight. I know my boys are in the back room of your shop," he was insisting despite the owner's protests. "You tell them that if they aren't home in ten minutes, I'll be there to get them—and no locks will stop me." Mark slammed down the receiver. He found his jacket, located his keys, and grabbed an axe. "I was in hell," Mark says.

"If my boys hadn't driven up just as I was walking out the door, I would have taken that axe and chopped down the door to that shop—for starters."

Mark and his wife, Christine, had seen incredible deterioration in their family in the last three years. The boys were never at home anymore. Threats of running away and angry fights had replaced those good times they had experienced together only a couple of summers before. Even their marriage was beginning to quake. It was only after several months of observing the family deteriorate that they began to suspect drugs as the root of their family problems.

The Family Disease

When the disease of chemical dependency claims a member of a family, it will be only a short time before the entire family becomes sick. Problems in relationships develop that a few months before would have been unheard of. Many parents are unaware of what's happening until the situation becomes a crisis, even though the symptoms and corresponding changes are predictable. It still may take a year or two before the parents suspect chemical dependency as the main problem. In this chapter we will discuss a number of the patterns that happen in families suffering from chemical dependency. Even more important, we will suggest a number of strategies for turning the family back to health.

A note on strategy before we begin. Changing people's behavior can be like pushing a string. We often get very unpredictable results. Teenagers are quick to spot our strategies and will become reactive and do just the opposite of what we would like them to do. For this reason, parents must be superstrategists. Like skilled chess players, we must be thinking many moves ahead to anticipate our children's countermoves. Even with our best efforts, however, parenting is not an exact science. Therefore, we must have a large repertoire of strategies, and we must be continually practicing our trade with the utmost skill. We must be innovative, always trying new things. And, as the old axiom says, "If it works, use it!" I have seen a great many parents, including the Oberts, take the challenge of parenting by the proverbial horns and come out with better results than they ever thought possible. The first step to finding the road to a healthy family is to understand some basic family dynamics.

The Need for Personal Space

Arguments over rules, chores, responsibilities, curfews, and personal space seem to dominate the agenda in families. To understand why, we first must look at the need each person has for personal space.

We all have a growing area of ownership that makes up our personal space. We often refer to it as our personal identity or self-image. We protect that space from all comers when we do not feel secure. That protective instinct causes us to do very destructive things to people who wander into our space and threaten us. The protective instinct is symbolized by the two arrows in figure 1.

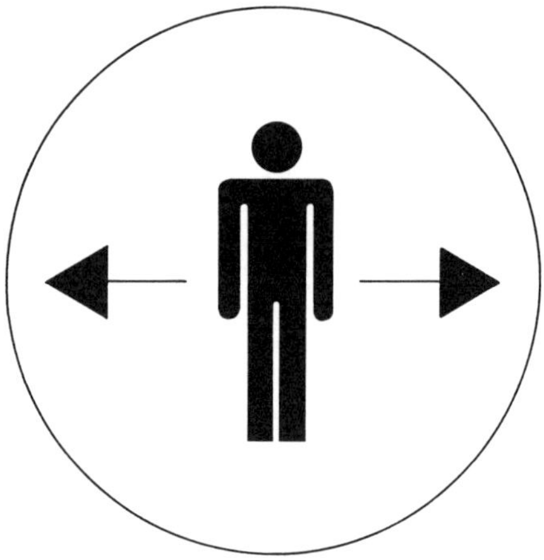

Figure 1. Personal space

The space varies in size, depending on our mood and how confident we feel about ourselves. When we are feeling defensive or threatened, the space will be very wide, and the force we use to push people out of that space will be very strong. When we are feeling confident, loving, and open, the personal space that we defend can be very small.

The size of someone's personal space also varies with age. A three-year-old does not need nearly as much space as a fifteen-year-old. It is in the teen years that the size of this space becomes the most volatile. Teens are expanding their space, trying to push the limits to see how far they can go for the least amount of cost to them personally. They can often expand their personal space to encompass such a large area that there is no way they can keep up with the requirements. They want the freedom but not the responsibilities. Just like kids who get up to a level of Space Invaders they cannot handle, teens who expand their space too quickly are sure to suffer devastating defeat.

Our job as parents is to teach our children how to expand their space slowly and with success. Then, if they choose to expand too quickly and go beyond their capabilities, they will have to learn from the school of hard knocks what the consequences are.

I like using an example from the game of Monopoly to teach teenagers about this principle. Many players get greedy and try to expand too quickly. They buy hotels and houses for their properties, only to land on an opposing player's property and have to sell their houses at half price to pay the rent. Teenagers do the same thing. They move out on their own without having a job. They buy stereos at 21 percent interest when they cannot even afford to eat. Or they go out and buy a five-thousand-dollar car with no thought for how they will pay for it in the end.

People who are not handling their own personal space effectively will have even more complications when someone else bumps up against that space, forming a relationship. Parents and other family members provide the chief threat to a teenager in this situation. If there are turf struggles (see figure 2), defenses will begin to rise as the arrows become larger and more intimidating. The individuals can quickly find themselves in a pushing match that invariably ends in one person's angrily leaving the room to protect his or her personal space. Teenagers who are abusing drugs will have no sensitivity to the people around them. Their quest for unlimited personal space can only be accomplished through deception and intimidation.

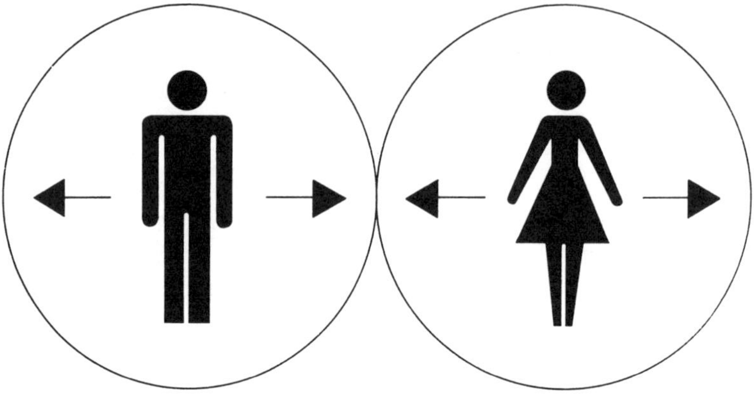

Figure 2. Personal spaces coming together in a relationship

"You get very creative and goal oriented to preserve your freedom to use drugs and do as you please," John says. "You learn to set your mind totally on your goal—which is to get and use drugs—and you make sure that nothing interferes with that goal."

"You develop a pretty good memory, too, so that you can get around your parents," Roger adds. "You sit around with your using friends, come up with a story together, then rehearse it again and again until everyone has it down. It takes a lot of effort to tell a pack of lies one day, then come up with a whole new pack of lies the next day—new lies that don't contradict the old lies you told the day before."

The Competing Need for Intimacy and Commitment—Family Space

As we all are painfully aware, leaving a situation does not make it better. In fact, most of the time it will greatly escalate the deterioration of the relationship. If personal space were our only need, this deterioration would not occur; however, we all have an equally strong, competing need: the need for intimacy and commitment. We need to be a part of other people's lives. We want to have someone to share with to keep us from being lonely. Ironically, that need for intimacy often flies in the face of our need for personal space.

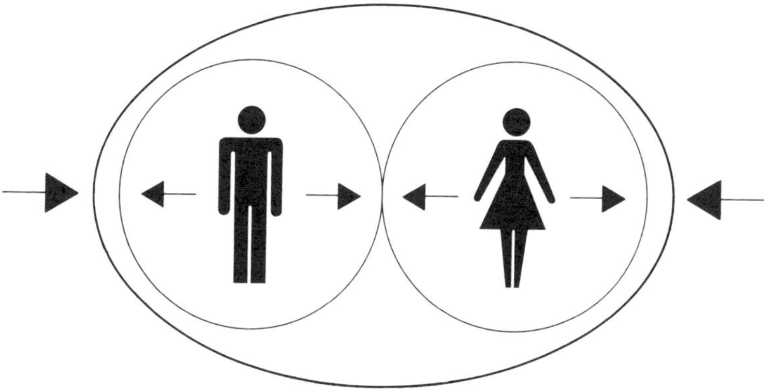

Figure 3. The double bind of personal relationships

Figure 3 shows the double bind of these two competing needs. The man's needs (dark arrows) are for personal space, but he also needs commitment from his female partner (outside dark arrow). This puts the woman in such a position that if she moves too quickly in either direction (toward more freedom or toward more intimacy), she could crash into his competing expectations and set off a battle. The man is caught in the same double bind.

How can we ever win? It seems as though we are condemned no matter which way we turn. The answer comes in finding a balance that both people become happy with. A healthy relationship is not necessarily one in which the parties are always close or always far apart. Rather, people with healthy relationships have learned to find a balance or a rhythm in which all parties are satisfied. Finding this balance is like learning how to dance. You have to establish a certain amount of closeness but also a certain amount of distance. Timing and sensitivity to your partner are essential. You must develop a rhythm in which you are close at the right times and can swing apart from each other at the right times. This makes building relationships a very difficult art. We like black-and-white answers, but the whole concept of health being a rhythm or a balance takes away the notion of easy answers and quick fixes.

The scientific term for this balance is *homeostasis.* It is a very important point that needs further exploration. Think about the systems of the human body. To be healthy, most systems need to be in balance. Take your body temperature, for instance: if it went up above 105 degrees Fahrenheit, you would find yourself in a severe medical emergency. On the other hand, if it dropped below 95 degrees Fahrenheit, you would also be in trouble. Your body acts like a thermostat, keeping your temperature from getting too high or too low. The same thing is true of respiration rate, blood pressure, heart rhythms, and just about every other system of the body.

We understand the concept of homeostasis, or balance, when we think about it in a physiological context; but when we start thinking about it in the context of family health and relationships, it can be more difficult to accept. We have a much greater tendency to see things as black or white, yes or no, when it comes to issues that are so personal and close to us. We need to discard this inclination and recognize the family's need for balance. Recognize, for example, that if you are continually pushing too hard for closeness, your teenager will likely continue striving for more distance. There must be a balance between the extremes. Both parties must be willing to work on it. And if one strategy does not bring about the balance that we desire, then we must get innovative and try something else.

Bipolarization

If conflict begins to build, the system will go out of balance, and we will begin to move apart from each other. We become opposites. Whether in a marriage relationship or a parent-child relationship, as conflict grows, we become more defensive and move away from the other person to protect ourselves. As conflict escalates, we become more and more the opposite of the other person. This process is called bipolarization.

Bipolarization occurs in several value spectrums that

affect the two people becoming opposites. In the financial spectrum, one becomes the penny-pincher, the other becomes the spendthrift. As religious conflict builds, the teen becomes more and more agnostic, the parent more and more dogmatic. As the parent gets more critical of long hair, the teen's hair gets longer and more bizzare. The more the parent hates rock music, the more drawn to it the teenager becomes.

Bipolarization also happens in the parents' relationship. As one parent becomes more suspicious and tough, the other one will often become more forgiving and permissive. Not understanding what the problem really is or what the solutions are, the parents can find themselves fighting more and drifting farther apart.

"The hardest thing for me to admit is that I wanted to opt completely out of the situation," Mark says. "I loved Christine. But I'd think about those top-level executives and stockbrokers who had left their fast life-styles to become beachcombers, and I envied them. I'd daydream about a place like that beach in Mexico, and as ashamed as I am to say this, I thought seriously about just taking off."

"Mark would tell me it was either John or him," Christine recalls. "What a position to be in. If I lost Mark, the boys would probably get completely out of control and leave home anyway. If I kicked John out, wouldn't that always be a barrier in my relationship with Mark? Any way I looked at it, I ended up with nothing."

"I would look at Christine," Mark continues. "I would really search for some flaw that could possibly help me justify leaving my family. But all I saw was a completely sweet, loving woman I'd never even argued with before this problem. No matter how bad it got, I finally decided I couldn't leave home, because I'd be leaving her."

The process of bipolarization can be illustrated by picturing two people who don't trust each other in a boat. For some reason, perhaps one is a prankster or just not a very good oarsman, one or both of the people begin to worry about turning the boat over. If the father, for instance, perceives that the son is starting to move toward the right side of the boat, invariably he will lean toward the left to make sure that the boat does not tip over. The son, feeling like his dad doesn't trust him, will often react by leaning even farther to the right. Each becomes more and more suspicious. Trust is gone on both sides. As each predictably leans more to his own side, the other is more convinced that his suspicions were warranted, and he justifies leaning to an even greater extreme.

You can imagine both of them eventually hanging off the main sail of this boat, straining as far they can to each of their sides just to keep the boat upright. A passerby could easily see both the problem and the solution. The solution is for both people to call a truce, sit down in the bottom of the boat, and get back to the task of trying to propel the boat toward whatever goal they have. But anyone who has ever tried to resolve a situation like this knows that getting both people to trust each other at the same time and move in toward the middle of the boat is a challenging task at best. Each one is reluctant to give up ground for fear that the other one will take advantage, or that the balance will be irreversibly moved toward the other person's position. This process accounts for the nuclear arms race, civil rights problems, lawsuits, and most marriage and family problems.

Again, the theory is simple. It is practicing the solution that is difficult. Both parties must recommit to renew their trust and come to a sensible balance. A truce must be called, and both must be able to sit down in the bottom of the boat and proactively discuss the situation and the possible solutions. When we let ourselves slip back into being reactive, the process of resolution is guaranteed to fail.

A key factor here is that there must be some agreement on the ground rules. The parties need to have some consensus on basic values and truths. This consensus can be achieved only after years of talking about what is important in the family and what is not. If these discussions have not taken place before the crisis, it is doubtful that common ground can be discovered in the heat of battle. Research shows pretty clearly that people from structured, religious backgrounds have fewer family breakups. I believe the reason is that they have a standardized value system that is usually written down—in scripture, for example—and can be referred to. That way there is less chance of parents or kids making up the rules of the game as they go along.

Despite having a consensus on ground rules and basic values, if a situation cannot be resolved by the parties, they might bring in an outside mediator. We easily lose perspective with family issues because they are so close to us. Involving a trusted outsider often helps us regain objectivity. Again, this person must be someone both parties trust.

Discussions need to take place in an environment that is conducive to good communication. Take time to find such a place. Go where you will be uninterrupted. Sit down to talk. Sit across from the other person so that you can see each other fully. Be comfortable. Speak directly to the person, don't talk "about" him or her. Use "I" messages, and talk about your feelings. Keep things as calm as possible. Keep your energy level up. If you start to get tired, call a recess and set up another specific time to meet again.

Don't debate facts. Get directly to the solution. What do you want to see changed? Ask the other person the same question: "What would you like to see changed?" That question can throw cold water on the best of argumentative fires. Often we just want to complain about the problem. Getting down to specific solutions can spoil the "fun" of a good argument.

Write things down so you can refer to them. Know what your minimum expectations are, and be clear in stating them. Be willing to negotiate on things that are not essential. Be fair, but don't sell out. Don't let the other person intimidate you or demand things; make him or her be proactive. And make sure you are proactive. Use some common sense rules of communication, and you will find the bipolarization begin to reverse itself. That brings us to another principle that can complicate communication problems in the family even more.

The Argument Spiral

We exchange our ideas and thoughts in what we normally call communication. Communication is the exchange of information back and forth from one person to another. This exchange could be depicted as a constant circle of information (see figure 4).

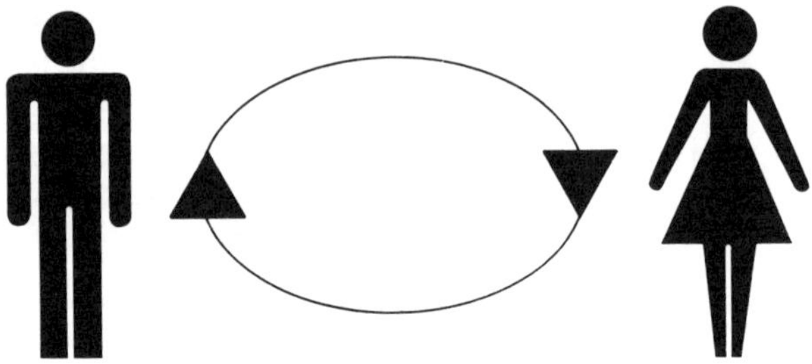

Figure 4. Communication: the circular flow of information between parent and child

The rhythm of that exchange of information must stay within a certain balance, or homeostasis, just as with personal space. If it gets going too quickly, people aren't listening to each other, and they tend to polarize from one another. If it goes too slowly, people eventually get bogged down and get angry, and soon someone leaves the room.

Figure 5 shows a communication circle that has gone out of control and spiraled into an argument. It might be helpful to put this argument on a ten-point scale. One to three symbolize communication that is within the balance and has not gone over the limit of control. People are agreeing to disagree, and there is some sense of balance. As the spiral climbs to four to six, we start to hear exaggerated terms such as *never* and *always,* typically prefaced by *you*. As the argument heats up to seven and eight, the whole relationship becomes unstable. Someone is going to leave. Accusations become much more critical, and the anger level gets out of control. At nine and ten the relationship explodes. People begin throwing things at each other, pushing, shoving, leaving rooms, and slamming doors. Almost every argument will wind up with at least one person angrily leaving the scene. Walking out of the room and slamming a door can be just as affrontive as staying to continue the argument.

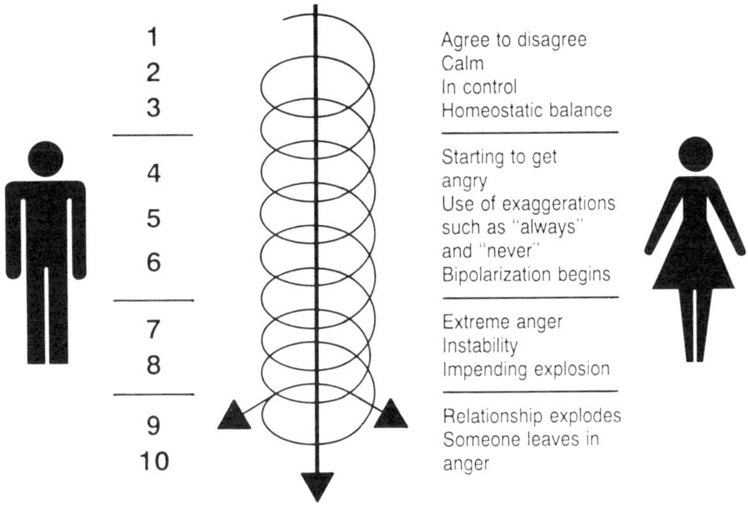

Figure 5. The argument spiral

We have all lost our temper at one time or another. We have all been in arguments. Being out of control is never good for the relationships or the individuals. Learning to stay within that homeostatic balance is critical in bringing a family back to a state of health.

It is my firm conviction that we should draw a line at three, drive a metal stake deep into that spot, and never allow ourselves to lose our tempers and go above that level. That is absolutely true with parents of a teenage drug user. If the parent loses control and says a lot of things that he or she really doesn't mean, all that will do is give the teen a tremendous amount of ammunition to use later. Another consideration is one of strategy and how you use your energy. As pointed out in chapter 7, we have only a limited amount of energy with which to get through the day. It is guaranteed that after you finish an argument that has gone up to eight or nine, you will feel exhausted and unable to function. An out-of-control parent serves as a great excuse for the teenager to rationalize continued drug use.

Equally dangerous is that we have broken our value system. We often feel guilt and regret about what we have said, so we go back to the teenager to make up and end up giving the kid a much better deal than he or she would have gotten before. Many teens are experts at playing this game. They get their parents pumped up by pushing all their buttons so that the parents fly out of control. Then they wait expectantly for their parents to come back feeling guilty so they will make a deal for the teenagers to get exactly what they wanted in the first place.

The rule, then, is to commit to stopping at three. Parents must learn self-control and ways to deal with their own tempers before they can develop good strategies for dealing with an alcohol- or drug-addicted child. And remember, you may not have much time. Anger is a choice. So is inner peace. You must decide now if you truly want the situation to improve. If you do, you must commit to staying cool and saving your energy for strategizing rather than for knock-down-drag-out fights.

Roles within the Family

One of the most interesting processes to watch in our children as they grow is the establishing of their individual identities. They form these identities by taking on different roles in the family and by modeling after people they admire. Chemical dependency will affect all aspects of the family, especially this role-taking process. When the family starts to go out of control, bipolarization and the argument spiral can create some effects damaging to other brothers and sisters.

Children in a family will naturally gravitate off into their own corners to find their unique personal space and identity. No matter how much parents might desire that their children have some sense of similarity, there will always be distinct differences between them because of this need to find a unique personal space. Each will find a specific role in the family that best suits him or her.

In almost every family, children will develop in one of three ways: conformer, nonconformer, and moderator. Sometimes this will be a first-, second-, and third-child phenomenon, but many times it will be contingent on the interaction patterns that evolve within the family. Conformers are kids who find their reward in staying within the family boundaries, living up to the expectations of the parents, and not doing a tremendous amount of questioning of rules that are imposed on them. It's not unusual for a first child to grow up with this kind of a pattern simply because there are two adult parents setting a rule system against one young child. If the parents are united at all in their parenting strategies, it's not hard to keep that first child in line.

If the next child comes within a period of two to three years, and especially if two are the same sex, it wouldn't be unusual for that child to take a dramatically different or opposite role from the conformer. The first child, who has a two-year jump on the younger one, is often tempted to portray his or her life-style as the only real, true way to live. So the second one will often grow up with a tremendous resentment against that first child's life-style. Conflict can then develop between the two children, and they will tend to polarize away from each other. If the first likes school and loves football, you can almost guarantee that the second one will dislike school and hate sports.

The amount of polarization is often contingent on how high the two children go up the argument spiral together. Constant knock-down-drag-out fights will escalate the amount of polarization that takes place between the two. It is important for parents to establish certain standards and expectations about how children resolve disputes. If you let them go uncontrolled, you will find more polarization among the children.

It's not unusual for a third child to become a moderator or a problem solver. This young person becomes the peacemaker, moving between the two other children, settling disputes, taking a hidden role between the other two distinct parties. Again, these roles may not take a first-, second-, third-child pattern, but you will usually see polarization into these three corners among all families.

The role that is typically the most problematic in regard to alcohol and drugs is the nonconformer. This child constantly tests the limits of his or her own personal space and the family's space. This kid questions all the rules and values of the family. It's very easy to negatively label that child as the troublemaker, the rebel, or the black sheep of the family, but that does not have to be the result.

If parents are strategic about their approach, they can head off the situation before it becomes too extreme. A very important thing to do with the nonconforming child is to legitimize his nonconformer role and try to shape it to be more productive. Pick out role models of leaders and family members who were nonconformers in their childhood and went on to become productive members of society. Talk with the child about how important it is for our society to have people who question and test the assumptions of society. Often these people grow up to be great scientists, attorneys, and, indeed, good church leaders. For instance, the nonconformers can be much more difficult to deal with in Sunday School class, but they tend to make stronger decisions about their own personal faith. Hence, they could go on to become more productive members of their church than the conforming children who have never made their own personal decision to commit to the organization. The real key with nonconformers is in trying to get them to work within certain limitations and expectations without feeling like they have sold out their own identity.

The differing roles in the family seem to be God's greatest test for us as parents. Techniques that seem to have worked with the first child almost invariably fail to work with the second child. And when we are able to regroup and find something that works with the second child, it will probably not work with the third child. But if we have in our bag of tricks a full repertoire of strategies for handling conformers, nonconformers, and moderators, we will have a much greater chance of being able to raise all three categories of children without significant problems.

The End-Run Principle

When a child is constantly testing the limits, values, and rules of the family, it is easy to let the argument spiral run out of control. When that happens, the teenager may start a pattern of push-pull arguments that increasingly polarizes him from the parents and may propel him outside the family. The more we try to correct the situation, the worse it seems to get. The more we try to pull the child back into the family, the more that child pulls away. This escalating is called the end-run principle and can be very dangerous.

I was visiting the Grand Canyon once. A mother I saw there was very fearful of heights, and her three-year-old seemed to detect it. In gleeful delight he would get up close to the edge and then run away from her when she tried to catch him. The more she chased him, the closer he got to the edge. Finally, tempers began to flare, and the situation got so extreme that someone else finally had to intervene to keep this child from accidentally going off the edge. The mother's out-of-control behavior and continued chasing could have been the very thing that pushed her child over the edge.

Kids know when they have beaten us. When they get outside our grasp, we may have few options left. We cannot let them be in control when this happens. Deciding on the best strategy to deal with the situation is a great challenge. Parents must decide whether to handle the deviation with a direct frontal attack or to pull back from the child in hopes that the kid will feel the loss and return.

The problem with a frontal attack is that it can often lead to a dangerous escalation in deviation. If the attack is not a comprehensive, successful effort, the teen will slip around the end when the parents aren't looking or have dropped their guard. The frontal attack can be an excellent strategy, but you must make sure that you have planned it out and have the greatest possible chance of winning. (See chapter 5 on intervention for detailed suggestions on the frontal attack.)

The situation can become especially bad if the parents are losing their tempers and going above a three in the argument spiral. When we are angry and out of control, we encourage needless resistance and deviation with our children. They will push more and deviate farther. It's very difficult for us to maintain that level of anger and intimidation, so ultimately we get tired and let down our guard.

Soon we are unable to patrol the perimeter of the family well enough, and we do not have the energy to enforce family rules. When our kids know that we have let down, they will take us to the wall every time. We must use strategy and not brute force.

"I tried everything," Mark Obert says. "I tried rage—even when I didn't feel enraged. I'd work myself up and even attempted to rip John's sweater off once, trying to scare him. But I was always detached, watching for the effect I was having on him. I had no effect.

"So I'd try reasoning with him. John always ended our debates with 'I just don't believe the same way you do, Dad.' It never worked.

"So I tried threatening to kick him out of the house. But I only did that because I knew Christine would never let me follow through. Finally, I tried laying on a guilt trip. I'd act hurt and wouldn't talk to him for days."

"That was the tactic we liked best," John says, including Roger in this response. "As long as he wasn't talking to us, we were completely free to come and go as we pleased. We really liked Dad's 'guilt trip.' "

I call this the end-run principle because it reminds me of the strategies I used as a quarterback in high school. We did everything we could to lure in the defensive end, just like our kids do to us. That defensive end's whole purpose in life is to keep players from getting around the end. If he turned us up the middle, we would generally get only a short distance. But if we could lure him in and get around his grasp, we had the chance to get many more yards and score a touchdown. Once our kids get around our defenses, they will be scoring touchdowns against us right and left.

One strategy I used as a quarterback was to run up right in the face of that defensive end and make him go one way or the other. If I could get him to zig when I zagged, I could invariably elude his grasp and make more yards. Our kids are expert manipulators; they know how to run right up into our faces and make us zig when they zag. They can vacillate from incredibly intense, aggressive, intimidating behaviors to looking pitiful or abused and on the verge of committing suicide because of us. They all follow the rule that whatever works, works. In other words, whatever they can get to work on us, they will use again and again.

As parents, if we are going to play the game, we have to become good defensive ends. We have to learn to stand our ground and to predict what kind of feints and fakes our children will make toward us. It's when they have made the end run successfully that we are brought to the most difficult parenting decision we will ever face.

Strategic Withdrawal

There comes a point where any frontal attack may backfire on us. Any movement on our part seems to amplify the child's deviation away from the family. The most difficult decision of parenting then has to be made. Can you withdraw yourself from the teenager and preserve the rest of the family? In many cases that is the only strategy that you have left. And you must make sure that the family survives. If the family and the parents deteriorate, there is nothing left to attract the child back to.

We have discussed strategic withdrawal several times already. It is the final stand. It must be done strategically and with great love and patience. Remember, the goal is to get the child to come back with a commitment to live a proactive, drug-free life. The purpose is not to give you the chance to get in the last word. It is not a tactic for vengeance.

Pulling back from your child and not allowing him or her to manipulate the family will be your most difficult parental intervention; however, I have seen very few families of chemically dependent teenagers successfully resolve their problems without having to go through strategic withdrawal several times. Like the defensive end who has the quarterback running up into his face, you must be willing to stand your ground and follow through with what you know to be right. Free agency dictates that your children must make their own decision about whether they will continue to be a part of your family. Most will back down and stay. You will have won the battle, but you must continue to build on the victory so you can win the war.

Some will not back down. It may take months before they understand what they have given up and decide to return to the family. Some will continue the end run until they are adults. Some will never return.

The main goal here is for the teenager to appreciate the family enough to want to continue to be a part of it. If the kid cannot commit to that, the family will do that child no good anyway. In fact, such a child will bring the rest of the family down with him or her. The rule that I find the most helpful comes from a teaching of Jesus in Mark 9:43, 47: "If thy hand offend thee, cut it off: it is better for thee to enter into life maimed, than having two hands to go into hell. . . . And if thine eye offend thee, pluck it out: it is better for thee to enter into the kingdom of God with one eye, than having two eyes to be cast into hell fire." In other words, if a part of you is beginning to kill the rest of your body, it is better to cut it off than to have the entire body die. We would all do absolutely everything we could do to treat that diseased member first. But if nothing seemed to work, we would have to preserve the larger body by cutting off the diseased member.

The beautiful difference here with families is that the teenager may turn out more like a prodigal than a diseased hand and return to you ready to become whole and healthy again. It is exhilarating to watch kids come back. Humbled, appreciative, they come back ready to work. If the interventions have been done in love, the chances are much more likely that they will return. When they come back with that kind of attitude, pull out the stops and let them know how much you love them. Remember the example of the prodigal son. After he had squandered his life and been humbled, he returned home. But his father did not greet him with a lecture; he embraced him and had a celebration. That kind of forgiveness can be a great attraction to bring a kid home, ready to get to work and put his or her life in order.

John and Roger both entered treatment programs after Mark and Christine gave them the ultimatum: "Stop using drugs, or you will no longer be able to live with your family." They are doing well and progressing toward proactive life-styles. As much as Mark and Christine may dread the thought of ever going back to that bottom line, "Shape up or ship out," they know they may have to in order to keep their family healthy. And in the long run that is exactly what both of these boys need in their recovery.

Chapter 10

COMMUNITY ACTION

"You've heard the philosophy that the way to raise kids is to 'catch them doing something right' and then praise them. I found myself asking neighbors, teachers, even the police, to help me catch Brandon 'doing something wrong' so that we could help him," Ralph Carlisle remembers.

Behind every drug-rehabilitated teenager—a kid who can now say no to drugs—are friends, or more likely parents, who had the courage to say yes.

"Yes—though I wish with all my heart it were otherwise—my son Brandon is addicted to drugs," says Suzanne Carlisle to an audience of silent parents. "And yes, Brandon's drug problem, by any name—chemical dependency, substance abuse, addiction—is a disease that we will live with for life." Her voice is strong, steady, and utterly void of shame. For the past two years Suzanne has devoted nearly all her time to sharing the power of saying yes with students, service or community groups, and church congregations.

Brandon's father, Ralph, is equally comfortable relating Brandon's drug story uncensored, letting society's judgments fall where they may.

"Police officers took Brandon out of his ninth grade class in handcuffs, drove him to the Bountiful police station, and interrogated him for half a day," Ralph Carlisle says. "Right away we knew something was wrong." He smiles at his punch line, knowing he's turned our focus onto the denial he experienced as a father. "Suzanne and

I aren't people who care much what others think of us," Ralph says. "And we did all the things people associate with good parenting. But Brandon did his best to redefine the limits of getting high."

Brandon was admitted into treatment, along with his whole family, when he was sixteen. His recovery included a long series of setbacks. For more than four months Brandon attempted, at times, to scam the program. But even though he kept using drugs occasionally, he saw less and less logic in doing so. Eventually, his treatment succeeded. Brandon found more satisfaction in helping others get off drugs and stay off drugs than he found in using them himself.

Brandon, a good-looking, confident young man who stands more than six feet tall, could pass for a student body president at any high school. He has now graduated from treatment and has turned his natural leadership abilities from dealing drugs to teaching kids how to stay off them. He works full-time as a chemical dependency technician, counseling youths like himself through the difficult process of getting straight.

Brandon and his parents have become crusaders, of a sort, against drug use. Suzanne's commitment to risk and share has resulted in her organizing literally hundreds of presentations to promote drug-free youth, becoming involved in local alliances of parents, and even, over the course of a year, caring for twenty-four recovering addicts in her home as part of Dayspring's host-home program. Ralph has taken copies of drug-awareness books to many neighbors and friends and has helped to raise funds for the Dayspring program.

When asked why they put so much of their time and effort into such a cause, they respond, "We have a son back." Brandon says with confidence, "And I feel like I've found my life's work."

The Carlisle story is one of thrilling success. And even though success has to be taken one day at a time, one of the surest ways to continue solid sobriety is to stay involved in helping others. The Carlisles had never seen themselves as people who would become crusaders for a cause, particularly a drug-abuse cause. But when a disease affects a whole family so deeply, it is not unusual for people to want to get involved in the larger cure.

This chapter deals with getting involved. You may already have been affected by the problem, or you may just be wanting to keep the problem out of your particular community. I feel strongly that action now will help us to prevent further spread of the disease in our schools, our churches, and our neighborhoods. Getting involved in your community can be one of the most rewarding experiences of your life; without a doubt it will also be one of the most demanding. Trying to change a larger community system such as a school, a church, or a neighborhood can require even more strategizing than changing your own family. The rest of this chapter will present some strategies that have been found by many to be the most successful in mobilizing a community.

Networking

A very important action you can take to stop drug abuse in your community is to get the parents and adults communicating regularly with one another. This process is called networking. One reason that kids beat us in the drug-abuse game is that they are networking daily with their using friends. They are always on the phone to one another talking and exchanging information. We adults, on the other hand, often find ourselves sitting in front of our televisions barricaded behind the walls of our houses and our fences, not wanting to deal with anyone else after work. We have lost our sense of being neighborhoods and communities because we don't work at talking with one another. In this day and age it is not unusual for us to be unable to name the neighbors who live within three or four houses of us, let alone really know them as friends. The first rule in drug treatment is that you must know your child's friends. Second, you must know the parents of your child's friends. Third, you must network with those other parents so that you can check up on your teenagers and not let them manipulate you.

Organizing a Group

With such organizations as churches and schools, the parents need to begin meeting regularly to discuss the potential problem. A wide-angle approach to the problem in one or several education seminars can be useful in raising the general knowledge of the population and identifying people who are particularly interested in the solution. But the key to building a good action network and actually changing things in the group is when four or five individuals identify themselves as a core group. These are usually people who have been affected by the problem or for other reasons have a strong interest in stopping drug abuse in their group.

The core group should meet three or four times to get to know one another and to establish a general action plan. In these first meetings it is important to quickly and clearly agree that there is a problem that needs to be solved. After that is established, the next step is to clearly move on to possible solutions. It is easy at this stage to get caught up in talking about the problem and fail to come up with any plans to solve it. A brainstorming session should be held to generate all kinds of ideas of things that could be tried to help resolve the problem. This session should be structured so that there is no criticism or lengthy discussion of ideas. The goal of brainstorming is to generate as many ideas as possible. After you have generated a lengthy list, schedule another meeting to pick out the top priorities and the most achievable goals.

Once you have made some concrete plans, your group will want to identify a second tier of people who want to get involved. This tier should consist of two different sets of people. The first set should be people who have a relatively strong personal commitment to the problem and to those who are organizing the solution and who would be willing to put in a fairly extensive amount of time on the project. The second group should be key people in the community and in your group who support you on this project but are generally too busy to make a continuing commitment of time. These people should be decision makers, people respected in the community. You could use them one to three times in various meetings to generate support by endorsing the program.

The most important thing about people who get involved with your project is that they must remain positive about the problem. When drug abuse strikes, it is very easy to become reactive and negative and bitter. Make it a rule that you never have the right to gripe about something unless you are willing to try to help change it. Keep a positive approach to the problem. If we become reactive and righteously indignant, we are not acting any more effectively than our druggie kids.

Intervention at School

There is no doubt that schools are a hotbed of drug exposure for kids. The environment in American education is changing rapidly. Kids have much more mobility than they have ever had. Fewer and fewer campuses are closed, so students are left pretty well on their own throughout most of the day.

A good administration continues to keep tight reins throughout the year. If drug-using patterns increase dramatically and school administrators are not quick to act, the school can slide toward anarchy very quickly. Just as in a family, the problem can go on undetected for many months. Like many moms and dads, school principals and vice-principals can often be caught with a serious attitude of denial. The responsibility then falls upon those who are informed and motivated to try to change things at that school.

Most administrators are eager for involvement from motivated, proactive, positive parents; however, they will all be cautious about their schools being labeled as having more serious drug problems than others. The best rule here is the Golden Rule: approach your school administrators in the same way you would like to be approached if you were being informed of your child's drug problem.

An important quality in someone who is intervening in a larger system is to have a long-term commitment. Let the administration know that this is something that may take two or three years to change. Most administrators do not want to get involved daily but want to be informed of all activities occurring in the school and usually like to be involved in the big events.

One good way of working with schools is a series of educational events aimed at the parents. These are usually sponsored through the PTA and occur about twice a year. Don't be discouraged if the first ones don't go very well; it may take two or three years before parents begin to recognize the event and see its benefits. Get the best speakers you possibly can. Make sure they are informed about drug abuse and agree with you philosophically. Try to give them a little guidance about what you are looking for. For an especially powerful meeting, bring in fairly well-known parents or community leaders who have been affected by the disease in their own families. Have them tell their personal stories and what they believe the solutions to be. Even stronger speakers are recovering teenagers from your area who feel comfortable sharing their own stories with your group. These meetings can be very moving, and they elicit a large response from the school community. It is important to have a follow-up meeting about a week later for those who are interested in getting involved. The follow-up meeting gives you an opportunity to identify another group of parents who may be interested in helping out with the cause.

From this larger group of parents, identify a core group to function as an advisory committee to the school administration. Most of the major changes in the school could be made from this group. If the group is accepted by the school administration, it could create a forum for ongoing dialogue to address the problems and their potential solutions. It is important to make sure that you have committed, positive parents on this committee. This group should meet at least monthly and be on call to be summoned whenever there is a pressing issue that the school administration should hear about. This group can also work at getting changes throughout the district by working with the school board.

Reaching the Students

The second level of action in the school is aimed at the students themselves. Two basic strategies exist for reaching the students: the shotgun approach and the rifle approach. With the first, you try to reach the entire student body. With the second, you aim at the smaller number of high-risk youth.

The main advantage of a large-scale educational approach is that you can reach large numbers of students without much expense. Drug and alcohol use is a hot issue in junior high and high schools; it is not unusual to get large turnouts at a conference or an assembly dealing with this topic. There are a number of pitfalls inherent in assemblies, however. Presentations should not be aimed at educating kids about kinds of drugs or paraphernalia. That only stimulates the students' curiosity and may even lead to experimentation. The presentation must be serious, with an emphasis on the fact that there is no such thing as responsible drug use of any kind. Testimonials from former users can be very good, as long as they don't sound like war stories. A war story is a recounting of past experiences as though they were adventures rather than regrettable events. Law enforcement officers can give excellent presentations as long as they stay away from too much drama about past events and avoid getting overpoweringly negative about the enforcement aspects. All subjects need to be approached with a matter-of-fact attitude. Emotions and drama need to be sincere and grow naturally out of personal experience. In assemblies you will want to have a high ratio of teachers to students. Students are often very rude to speakers, and there is a direct correlation between control and the number of teachers in the assembly. If used well, the large educational approach can create a snowball effect in the school; however, by itself a presentation in an assembly will seldom be enough of a base for such effect.

Small-group discussions tend to be much more powerful and long-lasting in their impact. An excellent technique is to follow up the big school assembly with small discussion groups led by teachers. School officials and parents should be ready to take on anything that comes from these meetings, however. It is not unusual to identify twenty-five to fifty kids who are in need of some sort of intervention. The school should allow several days for things to settle back down to normal. If things go extremely well, the school may want to start some sort of peer support group.

Peer support groups in schools are rapidly becoming a critically important intervention strategy. Many kids who know that they are beginning to develop a problem will seek out help from their friends. If a group is meeting after school or during the last period of the day to talk about such problems, it is easy to move a troubled child into that group. As the group members get to know one another and relationships begin to build, a spirit can grow that will allow the young people to support each other and confront one another when they start to get into problems. The ideal is to have the group include several recovering drug users from the school who have a commitment to help other young people escape from the problem.

The peer support group needs to be run by a teacher or an outside counselor in whom the school administration has confidence. Even more important, this person must have the kind of personality that will be accepted by the students; they have to feel comfortable enough to talk. At the same time, that leader must have enough strength to develop a group that can include both support and confrontation. Attendance at the group should be a privilege. Students who are not motivated to work on problems should not be allowed to continue to come. One way to make the group legitimate is to get the time period approved for credit. We've found that kids who are involved in such groups are much more likely to stay in school and perform well. They are also much more likely to recognize their drug problems earlier and be able to maintain a commitment to say no.

Some schools are using peer counseling programs. These can be excellent, but they can also be expensive to run and have to be supervised very closely. One problem with peer counseling programs is that often schools use straight kids to counsel druggie kids. It is very unusual to find a straight kid who will be accepted by the druggie kids. This approach can work, however, if you always have older kids counseling younger ones: that is, high school kids can counsel junior high students, and junior high kids can counsel children of elementary school age. It is usually more effective to find kids who are recovering themselves but have several months of sobriety and a strong commitment to staying straight. Any peer counseling program will be destroyed if members are allowed to use and the peer counselors are seen as hypocrites.

Church Groups

Another fruitful area for organizing a group may be your local church organization. Some excellent things are already being done in churches, but is important that drug abuse be addressed specifically. It is common for churches to think that they are immune to the problem and then have it break out in a number of their young people.

A parents group at a church needs to have several specific goals. The first is to increase people's knowledge about drugs and alcohol. The second is to teach the basic skills and dynamics of parenting so parents can have a better chance of preventing the problem. The third is to form an ongoing support group for parents who have identified specific problems they need help with.

A youth group at a church also needs several specific goals. First, educate the young people better. Make it a habit to discuss drug abuse four or five times a year. Second, start a support group for young prodigals who are on their way to recovery. Many churches host AA and NA meetings in their buildings with great success. These young people can be instrumental in keeping kids from getting involved in the first place. Younger kids tend to listen to them much better than they listen to adults.

Soon these recovering kids will start to feel that they are doing something vital and essential to the functioning of their church. The more ownership they feel, the more investment they make. The more invested they get in meaningful activities such as this, the less chance there is that they will suffer relapse.

Conclusion

Many times a program is secondary to the personalities involved. I cannot stress too much the effect one person can have in making or breaking a prevention program. People who get negative and reactive and lose their tempers may be able to create change in the short run, but they do not establish programs that last. That's why our groups need to be " Students For . . ." and "Parents For . . ." instead of "Students Against . . ." and "Parents Against . . . ."

It is amazing to me how much difference one person can make by putting together a movement that can eventually change an entire state; however, you must start out with your own small area. Each small group needs to attract several committed core people for the movement to continue.

Fortunately for the movement, you will find dozens of parents who will give their hearts and souls to help save other children from the menace of drug abuse. Many of these parents will donate hundreds of hours of volunteer service to try to save another young person from this disease.

The battle will be won not by media campaigns but in the trenches, from child to child, house to house, and school to school. The media attention and commitments of our leaders and celebrities help to bring focus and legitimacy to the movement, but the battle will be won only when we are willing to square off with another person face to face and ask that person to commit to a drug-free life.

Chapter 11

HOPE FOR THE FUTURE

There are no easy solutions to the problem of drug and alcohol abuse. Neither are there foolproof preventive measures a family can take or religious answers that will work in every instance. Those are the cold realities of the world in which we live. But there is warmth here, too, and hope, and possibilities for raising your chances of keeping your children drug free. Most of all, there are parents who understand what you might be going through, because they've been there, too. I asked some of these parents, whose kids are in treatment at Dayspring, to share their feelings in answer to the question: "If you were going to say one thing to other parents about the drug problem and its solution, what would it be?" Here are some of their responses:

"Get educated. Find out what is going on out in the world with your kids. Know what to look for and what to do if it happens in your home."

"Don't let your family be destroyed by one member. . . . Sometimes you have to hurt to show real love."

"This disease doesn't have to be the worst thing that has happened to your child—with treatment, your child can achieve more growth and self-knowledge and spiritual commitment than many straight kids get. A terrible thing can become the means for a fine outcome."

"Don't ever think it can't happen to your child. No one is safe from alcohol and drugs."

"Love your children enough to give them what they need, and that is not always what they want. If you have that courage, there is light at the end of a very long tunnel."

"Lying and denial are automatic by-products of drug use. Kids need help to understand the problem and overcome it."

"Love your kids, keep the communication open, get educated about drugs, and if you have a kid in trouble, don't let your pride interfere with getting help for him or her. It may mean the difference between whether your kid has a future or not."

"Freedom, love, prayer, and honesty—these principles are really the only way to lasting change."

Lasting change is not an impossible hope. As we learn about the changing world and the new challenges and problems our kids are confronted with, we can arm ourselves against those challenges and make a difference. As we admit our own frailties and problems, we can open ourselves to help from others. As we learn to reach out—to our children, to our neighbors, to our world—we can break the communication barriers that block out hope and meaning for so many. And as we rely on strength far beyond our own, we can effect changes we never thought possible. Ours may never be a drug-free world, but we can do everything in our power to make sure that our families lead a drug-free existence.

Appendix

DRUGS OF ABUSE

Drugs can generally be separated into different categories according to the effects that they have on the human body and mind. There are depressants, stimulants, hallucinogens, and painkillers. Kids typically experiment with different kinds to get different effects. Although some will take you up and some will take you down and some will take you into a hallucinatory world, I still believe that "a drug is a drug is a drug." The addiction cycle is similar in them all. And when we look at the deterioration of the teenager's mind, body, and spirit, all of the drugs look the same. It is critical for parents to become educated about all the drugs. The information in this appendix will help you become familiar with the major categories of drugs and their names, but if you have a child who is abusing drugs, you should consult a text that covers the subject in greater depth. (See Suggested Reading on p. 161.) Consult the table below for a brief summary of the categories, effects, and common names of drugs.

Depressants

Depressant drugs are those that bring your mood and energy level down. The main euphoric effect that teenagers seek by using depressant drugs is the feeling of being relaxed and mellow. This category is by far the largest category of abuse. Most teenagers are looking to get high by relaxing and forgetting about the cares of their everyday world. Depressants help the user drop inhibitions and anxieties and allow him or her to become more gregarious at social gatherings. People who are normally uptight find themselves able to make new friends and "be crazy" and maybe for the first time in their lives be able to make people laugh. It is sad that kids feel they have to be drugged to take on these qualities, especially when the reality is that drugs don't do anything for them that they could not experience naturally, drug free.

Alcohol is the most commonly used depressant drug worldwide. No matter what beverage it is, whether beer, wine, or distilled liquor, the ethanol (alcohol) is the same active ingredient in all substances. The rule of thumb is that one ounce of distilled liquor contains the same amount of alcohol as an eight-ounce glass of wine or a twelve-ounce can of beer. At the early stages of intoxication, alcohol will block memories of impending tasks or unpleasant events that are in the teenager's future. It relaxes inhibitions and allows the kid to party while feeling high. At later stages of intoxication, the body attempts to remove this chemical, which it sees as a poison. It will try to reject the drug by causing the teenager to vomit. If this rejection didn't happen, the alcohol could create an overdose. The long-term damage done by alcohol is primarily to organs that eliminate or process the substance. The heart, the liver, and the stomach are prime targets for alcohol's degenerative effects. Alcohol is so widespread and so easily available that very few chemically dependent teenagers fail to identify it as one of their top three drugs.

Marijuana is a difficult drug to classify. It has some long-term depressant characteristics that help to modify mood and take away anxieties, but it also has some mild hallucinogenic characteristics. The drug looks like chopped-up oregano. Leaves can be either green or brown. Marijuana is usually stored in plastic sandwich bags; however, kids also use a small container such as a 35mm film container. The drug is generally sold for personal use in grams or "eighths" (one-eighth of an ounce), which usually sell for about fifteen dollars. That amount would likely last up to three days for a teen with a daily habit; however, it's not unusual for adolescents at Stage Four to be smoking an eighth a day.

The effects of marijuana are very slow, making it difficult to detect its use in a teenager. They are also quite long-term. Marijuana has a half-life of twenty-four to forty-eight hours. The half-life is the time it takes for a drug to go from full strength to half strength in the body. For example, it takes about two days for four grams of marijuana to drop to two grams in the bloodstream. Alcohol, on the other hand, has a half-life of three to four hours. It is eliminated much more quickly from the system, but it has a greater potential for abuse and overdose. The potential for overdose of marijuana is very low. A drug with a similar half-life is valium. It is very difficult to detect valium use in a fellow employee or a neighbor unless you watch their slow deterioration in performance over a period of several months.

The research on the adverse effects of marijuana is still coming in; however, there is no doubt that marijuana use is extremely detrimental to the lungs, the heart, and the vascular system. Pot contains more carcinogens than cigarettes, the smoke is hotter, and the smoke is taken into the lungs and held for as long as possible. The smoke alone makes marijuana much harder on the lungs than cigarettes. There is also significant evidence to show that marijuana retards hormonal development and affects the body's immune system. The recent upswing in immunologically based diseases such as AIDS and herpes is often correlated with heavy marijuana use.

Marijuana is stored in the fat cells. The organ in the human body that contains the highest percentage of fat is the brain. One of the most disconcerting effects that marijuana has on the brain is that it deteriorates short-term memory. Our brains store a tremendous amount of information in short-term memory before prioritizing it and logging it into long-term memory. Consequently, we all forget a lot of things that we see only one time. A marijuana abuser, however, will have much more serious difficulty trying to remember things after one exposure. Kids in treatment for heavy marijuana use often have serious reading disabilities. They begin to read a chapter and forget the title of the chapter. They read the first page, and by the time they go on to the second page they have forgotten what the first page was about. They soon become discouraged at their inability to perform mental tasks and eventually develop an apathy syndrome. The most predictable effect of marijuana abuse is a slow deterioration over several months in the teenager's ability to perform specific, evaluated mental exercises. So you can guess that the first area to go is school. In our highly technical society, where learning is a survival skill, this combination spells the kiss of death for a teenager's future.

Other depressant drugs that teenagers abuse include various forms of tranquilizers and sleeping medications. Kids will often dig around in the medicine cabinet to find Mom's valium prescription that has sat there for years or those sleeping pills that Dad used to take when he was younger. Parents should clean out their medicine cabinet and lock up anything that has potential for abuse.

Another type of very destructive depressant is inhalants. An inhalant is defined as any gaseous substance that can be inhaled into the lungs and absorbed into the bloodstream, where that gas takes the place of oxygen. As the brain is starved for oxygen, the user begins to feel lightheaded, achieving an overall depressant effect. Just about anything in an aerosol can can be inhaled. Different chemicals in this category that might be abused are glue, gasoline, paint, nonstick cooking spray, hair sprays, and even the aerosol from whipped cream cans. Anything that produces a gaseous fume can be inhaled and get a kid high. The problem is that brain cells that are starved for oxygen die after about five seconds. Most kids know that inhalants can cause brain damage; therefore, most of the abuse of inhalants takes place among kids who cannot get any other drugs. Such kids include very young adolescents, lower-income kids, and those from rural areas where drug supplies are periodic. That doesn't mean, by the way, that abusable drugs are not available in rural areas. The most recent studies show that rural areas are closing the gap that has existed for the last ten years. It's just that typically the flow of drugs is less reliable in rural areas, and the rural child may have to get high on whatever is available during the times of drug drought.

Stimulants

Stimulant drugs are uppers. Because they make your brain respond faster, or speed up, the most commonly abused drugs in this category are called speed. Several groups exist in this category. The most sought after come from the family of drugs called amphetamines. Generally these are prescription drugs prescribed for appetite suppression and weight loss. Another common use is for the treatment of hyperactive children. Children who are hyperkinetic chemically will have a paradoxical reaction to speed. The drug will slow them down and allow them to perform more functionally at school and home. The real problem is that many kids are misdiagnosed as being hyperactive or as having Attention Deficit Disorder (ADD). These kids are usually teenagers, and they know they can get big money for their drugs on the street.

Another common form for speed is in a white tablet called a cross top. These are drugs manufactured in clandestine, underground laboratories. Their content is often very questionable. Many of them contain only decongestants and mild stimulants a little more powerful than caffeine. The danger in these is that a teenager will get used to taking eight to ten to feel some kind of a buzz, and then will come across real speed. A teenager who takes eight to ten amphetamines will have a serious overdose that might easily result in death.

A very powerful form of stimulant is called methamphetamine. The street name for this drug is crank (not to be confused with crack, which is a form of cocaine described below). Crank is often snorted or injected and provides a much more intense speeding sensation, or rush. Because the effects are faster and more extreme, the drug has extreme potential for abuse and overdose.

Cocaine is rapidly becoming the drug of choice for a

growing number of teenagers. The drug provides a significant stimulatory experience as well as some hallucinogenic effects. The drug is typically snorted in powder form, but it can also be smoked or shot up.

Crack is the latest form of cocaine. It is cocaine that has been chemically transformed into a more potent form that can be smoked. The smoking potential is attractive to drug users because the experience is much more intense than snorting, and they don't have to resort to a needle to shoot up. Smoking a drug will cause it to be absorbed by the lungs, so it works faster and requires less of the drug to get the person high. That means that the cost per dose goes down and puts the drug within the financial reach of more teenagers.

Cocaine has a significant potential for overdose. It is very difficult to control how much of the drug you actually absorb into your bloodstream. It takes only a few seconds to absorb the drug when it is smoked in the form of crack. Although it provides a very stimulating, peak experience in a short time, it is also followed by a very sudden and predictable drop-off in mood as the drug wears off. With any stimulant drug, there is almost always a period after drug use in which the user crashes. The drug produces a tremendous craving and addiction by itself, but the threat of crashing afterwards makes it even more imperative to find more of the drug. The most serious side effect of cocaine abuse is irregularity of the heartbeat (arrhythmia). More and more apparent heart-attack victims are showing up in emergency rooms and intensive care. Often these victims turn out to be young people suffering from cocaine overdose. The recent deaths of several celebrities have been clear examples of the dangers of cocaine overdose.

Another serious drawback of cocaine is the expense. Currently one gram of cocaine (about the equivalent of a two-inch stick of chalk) costs about one hundred twenty dollars. Tolerance to cocaine develops very rapidly. It's not unusual for people who are in the later stages of chemical dependency to spend a thousand dollars a day on the drug. Still another adverse effect of cocaine is that long-term abuse of any stimulant can create a form of psychosis.

Cocaine users start to lose touch with reality and almost always become paranoid. They start to have hallucinations and might become suicidal in the midst of one of these episodes. But as with all drugs, the major problems are behavioral. People on cocaine can go through the four stages of the disease in a matter of weeks. It's not unusual for them to sink themselves into debt twenty or thirty thousand dollars. All stimulants have serious potential for abuse.

Hallucinogens

Hallucinogenic drugs produce a distortion in the senses. The electrical impulses of the brain seem to be thrown out of synchronization. People see smells and hear colors. Inanimate objects become animated. The senses all become heightened. The major drug of abuse in this category is LSD (or acid). LSD dropped in popularity during the seventies but has had quite a revival during the eighties. LSD usually comes in the form of small pieces of paper or stamps about one centimeter square. These are often printed with pictures of pyramids, unicorns, or comic book characters. They are eaten and absorbed into the blood through the stomach. LSD can also come in tiny pills about the size of a BB called microdots.

A typical acid trip will last anywhere from four to twelve hours. The teenager who has used this drug regularly and learned how to control the effects can usually maintain at school or within the family without being detected. The primary danger of LSD is that it creates a synthetic psychosis. For many kids who are experiencing emotional problems anyway, this artificially induced psychosis can be too stressful. Many never return to their original mental state. If used regularly over a long period of time, LSD can have significant effects on brain function.

A common nickname for LSD among the kids is fry. This name is based on their assumption that if you use LSD for a long period of time, you will fry your brain. Kids in our clinic who have abused a significant amount of LSD will show a much greater propensity toward psychosis. Some people suggest that psychotic people tend to abuse

LSD more, but I am convinced that the LSD has caused them to lose their perspective on what is real and what is not.

Another significant problem with LSD is that it takes only a microscopic amount to equal one unit dose. LSD is always made in clandestine laboratories, which do not have a great reputation for quality assurance, and a dose in one hit may be three to five times greater than in the next.

Another significant hallucinogen is phencyclidine (PCP, also called angel dust). This drug could also be classified as a tranquilizer because it was originally developed for veterinary use in putting animals to sleep while they were operated on. When used by humans it has drastic emotional effects. People on PCP might vacillate from being incredibly depressed to being totally outraged. It also has the effect of working partially as an anesthetic and makes users somewhat impervious to pain while they are on it. Numerous examples could be cited of kids who were high on PCP requiring six or seven adult men to subdue them. There have also been instances of kids pulling their hands through handcuffs and stripping back all the flesh from their bones.

The word has been out about PCP for a long time. Back in the sixties the flower children were aware of it but typically steered away from it because it was considered to be a bad drug. It made a comeback at the beginning of the eighties but quickly fell out of favor with kids because of the drastic emotional effects. The real danger is that many dealers spray PCP on pot or pass it off as other drugs. It is fairly easy and cheap to make and when substituted for another drug provides large profits to the dealer while offering a significant kick to the drug user.

The most significant adverse effect of PCP is that a number of people who use it become instantly psychotic. Two incidents at our facility in the past year were with young people who were given PCP and went totally out of control. Both had to be physically restrained and admitted to psychiatric hospitals. In both cases it was approximately a week before the acute psychotic symptoms began to subside; one of the kids took over six months to return to normal. Neither one of these kids had had any previous symptoms of psychosis before taking PCP.

Most of the kids know that PCP is a really bad drug. When they are buying street drugs, however, most will have little idea of what garbage drugs will have been mixed in to increase the profits of the dealer.

Painkillers

Narcotic painkillers are usually considered the hardest of hard-core drugs. Heroin, the granddaddy of them all, is derived originally from the opium plant and then distilled from morphine. The morphine-based drugs are typically shot up and provide quick physiological addiction for the user. This form of addiction still exists with teenagers, but most of them abuse painkillers that come from the codeine derivatives. Codeine is another product of opium. It usually comes in pill form and, as with all narcotics, is controlled by prescription. Drugs such as Percodan, Percocet, Tylenol 3, Tylox, and Darvon are all readily available and provide serious potential for abuse.

Parents should make sure that any prescribed painkiller is kept under tight lock and key and is never made available to a teenager except under the strictest doctor's orders. Many kids who have had several operations and experienced painkillers will turn back to them as their drug of choice. Some will come across them on the street, but a person who gets into painkillers gets into the most strictly controlled area of drugs and suffers the greatest potential of being arrested. Painkillers work as a depressant and tend to remove any feeling of pain from the mind. Because they are a depressant, they have high potential for overdose. Painkillers can prove very dangerous when taken with any other drug. Combining drugs creates a deadly synergy: one painkiller plus one depressant could add up to three to five doses' worth of either drug. As with any depressant, the risk with narcotic overdose is that the drug will shut down systems until it eventually gets to the midbrain and shuts down the heart or the lungs, killing the user.

In summary, "a drug is a drug is a drug." Each drug

has some unique properties, but the progression of the disease of drug abuse is similar in all people. Chemically dependent adolescents seldom recognize the dangerous state they are in, and when they do, they are so fearful of the results of coming forward that they seldom take the initiative to seek help. To arrest the disease there must be outside intervention from someone who cares.

Drugs	Trade or Other Names	Medical Uses
NARCOTICS		
Opium	Dover's powder, Paregoric, Parepectolin	Analgesic, antidiarrheal
Morphine	Morphine, Pectoral Syrup	Analgesic, antitussive
Codeine	Codeine, Empirin Compound with Codeine, Robitussin A-C	Analgesic, antitussive
Heroin	Diacetylmorphine, Horse, Smack	Under investigation
Hydromorphone	Dilaudid	Analgesic
Meperidine (Pethidine)	Demerol, Pethadol	Analgesic
Methadone	Dolophine, Methadone, Methadose	Analgesic, heroin substitute
Other Narcotics	LAAM, Leritine, Levo-Dromoran, Percodan, Tussionex, Fentanyl, Darvon*, Talwin*, Lomotil	Analgesic, antidiarrheal, antitussive
DEPRESSANTS		
Chloral Hydrate	Noctec, Somnos	Hypnotic
Barbiturates	Amobarbital, Phenobarbital, Butisol, Phenoxbarbital, Secobarbital, Tuinal	Anesthetic, anticonvulsant sedative, hypnotic
Glutethimide	Doriden	Sedative, hypnotic
Methaqualone	Optimil, Parest, Quaalude, Somnafac, Sopor	Sedative, hypnotic
Benzodiazepines	Ativan, Azene, Clonopin, Dalmane, Diazepam, Librium, Serax, Tranxene, Valium, Verstran	Antianxiety, anticonvulsant, sedative, hypnotic
Other Depressants	Equanil, Miltown, Noludar, Placidyl, Valmid	Antianxiety, sedative, hypnotic

*Not designated a narcotic under the CSA

Drugs	Trade or Other Names	Medical Uses
STIMULANTS		
Cocaine†	Coke, Flake, Snow	Local anesthetic
Amphetamines	Biphetamine, Delcobese, Desoxyn, Dexedrine, Mediatric	Hyperkinesis, narcolepsy, weight control
Phenmetrazine	Preludin	Hyperkinesis, narcolepsy, weight control
Methylphenidate	Ritalin	Hyperkinesis, narcolepsy, weight control
Other Stimulants	Adipex, Bacarate, Cylert, Didrex, Ionamin, Plegine, Pre-Sate, Sanorex, Tenuate, Tepanil, Voranil	Hyperkinesis, narcolepsy, weight control
HALLUCINOGENS		
LSD	Acid, Microdot	None
Mescaline and Peyote	Mesc, Buttons, Cactus	None
Amphetamine Variants	2,5-DMA, PMA, STP, MDA, MMDA, TMA, DOM, DOB	None
Phencyclidine	PCP, Angel Dust, Hog	Veterinary anesthetic
Phencyclidine Analogs	PCE, PCPy, TCP	None
Other Hallucinogens	Bufotenine, Ibogaine, DMT, DET, Psilocybin, Psilocyn	None
CANNABIS		
Marijuana	Pot, Acapulco Gold, Grass, Reefer, Sinsemilla, Thai Sticks	Under investigation
Tetrahydrocannabinol	THC	Under investigation
Hashish	Hash	None
Hashish Oil	Hash Oil	None

†Designated a narcotic under the CSA

Drugs	Physical Dependence	Psychological Dependence	Tolerance
NARCOTICS			
Opium	High	High	Yes
Morphine	High	High	Yes
Codeine	Moderate	Moderate	Yes
Heroin	High	High	Yes
Hydromorphone	High	High	Yes
Meperidine (Pethidine)	High	High	Yes
Methadone	High	High	Yes
Other Narcotics	High-Low	High-Low	Yes
DEPRESSANTS			
Chloral Hydrate	Moderate	Moderate	Possible
Barbiturates	High-Moderate	High-Moderate	Yes
Glutethimide	High	High	Yes
Methaqualone	High	High	Yes
Benzodiazepines	Low	Low	Yes
Other Depressants	Moderate	Moderate	Yes
STIMULANTS			
Cocaine†	Possible	High	Possible
Amphetamines	Possible	High	Yes
Phenmetrazine	Possible	High	Yes
Methylphenidate	Possible	High	Yes
Other Stimulants	Possible	High	Yes
HALLUCINOGENS			
LSD	None	Degree unknown	Yes
Mescaline and Peyote	None	Degree unknown	Yes
Amphetamine Variants	Unknown	Degree unknown	Yes
Phencyclidine	Degree unknown	High	Yes
Phencyclidine Analogs	Degree unknown	Degree unknown	Yes
Other Hallucinogens	None	Degree unknown	Possible
CANNABIS			
Marijuana	Degree unknown	Moderate	Yes
Tetrahydrocannabinol	Degree unknown	Moderate	Yes
Hashish	Degree unknown	Moderate	Yes
Hashish Oil	Degree unknown	Moderate	Yes

†Designated a narcotic under the CSA

Drugs	Duration of Effects	Usual Methods of Administration
NARCOTICS		
Opium	3–6 hours	Oral, smoked
Morphine	3–6 hours	Oral, injected, smoked
Codeine	3–6 hours	Oral, injected
Heroin	3–6 hours	Injected, sniffed, smoked
Hydromorphone	3–6 hours	Oral, injected
Meperidine (Pethidine)	3–6 hours	Oral, injected
Methadone	12–24 hours	Oral, injected
Other Narcotics	Variable	Oral, injected
DEPRESSANTS		
Chloral Hydrate	5–8 hours	Oral
Barbiturates	1–16 hours	Oral, injected
Glutethimide	4–8 hours	Oral, injected
Methaqualone	4–8 hours	Oral, injected
Benzodiazepines	4–8 hours	Oral, injected
Other Depressants	4–8 hours	Oral, injected
STIMULANTS		
Cocaine†	1–2 hours	Sniffed, injected
Amphetamines	2–4 hours	Oral, injected
Phenmetrazine	2–4 hours	Oral, injected
Methylphenidate	2–4 hours	Oral, injected
Other Stimulants	2–4 hours	Oral
HALLUCINOGENS		
LSD	8–12 hours	Oral
Mescaline and Peyote	8–12 hours	Oral, injected
Amphetamine Variants	Up to days	Oral, injected
Phencyclidine	Variable	Smoked, oral, injected
Phencyclidine Analogs	Variable	Smoked, oral, injected
Other Hallucinogens	Variable	Oral, injected, smoked, sniffed
CANNABIS		
Marijuana	2–4 hours	Smoked, oral
Tetrahydrocannabinol	2–4 hours	Smoked, oral
Hashish	2–4 hours	Smoked, oral
Hashish Oil	2–4 hours	Smoked, oral

†Designated a narcotic under the CSA.

Drugs	Possible Effects	Effects of Overdose	Withdrawal Syndrome
NARCOTICS			
Opium Morphine Codeine Heroin Hydromorphone Meperidine (Pethidine) Methadone Other Narcotics	Euphoria, drowsiness, respiratory depression, constricted pupils, nausea	Slow and shallow breathing, clammy skin, convulsions, coma, possible death	Watery eyes, runny nose, yawning, loss of appetite, irritability, tremors, panic, chills and sweating, cramps, nausea
DEPRESSANTS			
Chloral Hydrate Barbiturates Glutethimide Methaqualone Benzodiazepines Other Depressants	Slurred speech, disorientation, drunken behavior without odor of alcohol	Shallow respiration, cold and clammy skin, dilated pupils, weak and rapid pulse, coma, possible death	Anxiety, insomnia, tremors, delirium, convulsions, possible death
STIMULANTS			
Cocaine† Amphetamines Phenmetrazine Methylphenidate Other Stimulants	Increased alertness, excitation, euphoria, increased pulse rate and blood pressure, insomnia, loss of appetite	Agitation, increase in body temperature, hallucinations, convulsions, possible death	Apathy, long periods of sleep, irritability, depression, disorientation
HALLUCINOGENS			
LSD Mescaline and Peyote Amphetamine Variants Phencyclidine Phencyclidine Analogs Other Hallucinogens	Illusions and hallucinations, poor perception of time and distance	Longer, more intense trip episodes, psychosis, possible death	Withdrawal syndrome not reported
CANNABIS			
Marijuana Tetrahydro-cannabinol Hashish Hashish Oil	Euphoria, relaxed inhibitions, increased appetite, disoriented behavior	Fatigue, paranoia, possible psychosis	Insomnia, hyperactivity, and decreased appetite occasionally reported

† Designated a narcotic under the CSA

Source: Drug Enforcement Administration, U.S. Department of Justice, July 1979

SUGGESTED READING

Prevention

These books deal with how to approach the problem of drugs and alcohol in the early stages. They will give you an overview of strategies you can try in your school, church, community, or family.

Crowley, James F. *Alliance for Change: A Plan for Community Action on Adolescent Drug Abuse.* Minneapolis: Community Intervention, 1984.

Parents, Peers and Pot. Rockville, Md.: National Institution on Drug Abuse, 1979.

Prevention Plus: Involving Schools, Parents, and the Community in Alcohol and Drug Education. Rockville, Md.: National Institute on Alcohol Abuse and Alcoholism, 1983.

What Works: Schools without Drugs. Washington, D.C.: U.S. Department of Education, 1986.

Information about Drugs

These books provide specific information about the nature of drugs and alcohol and their effects.

For Parents Only: What You Need to Know about Marijuana. Rockville, Md.: National Institution on Drug Abuse, 1980.

Jones, Hardin, and Helen Jones. *Sensual Drugs.* Cambridge: Cambridge University Press, 1977.

Jones, Kenneth, Louis W. Shainberg, and Curtis O. Byer. *Drugs and Alcohol.* New York: Harper & Row, 1979.

The Disease of Addiction

These books help you understand the disease of addiction and what to do about it.

Johnson, Vernon E. *I'll Quit Tomorrow*. San Francisco: Harper & Row, 1980.

Polson, Beth, and Miller Newton. *Not My Kid*. New York: Avon, 1984.

Parenting

Parents must come up with new strategies. These books help to give you solid suggestions for things to try with your children.

Dinkmeyer, Donald. *Raising a Responsible Child*. New York: Simon and Schuster, 1973.

Glenn, H. Steven. *Developing Capable Young People*. Hurst, Tex.: Humansphere, n.d.

York, Phyllis, David York, and Ted Wachtel. *Toughlove*. New York: Bantam, 1982.

AA Standard Works

These two books are essential reading to understand the philosophy and history of the AA twelve-step approach to recovery from alcohol or drug addiction.

Alcoholics Anonymous. 3d ed. New York: Alcoholics Anonymous World Services, 1976.

Twelve Steps and Twelve Traditions. New York: Alcoholics Anonymous World Services, 1981.

Index